WHITE PRIVILEGE

essential readings on the other side of racism

EDITION

Paula S. Rothenberg
William Paterson University of New Jersey

WORTH PUBLISHERS

Senior Publisher: Catherine Woods
Acquisitions Editor: Sarah Berger
Marketing Manager: Lindsay Johnson
Marketing Coordinator: Jennifer Bilello
Art Director: Babs Reingold
Cover Designer: Kevin Kall
Interior Designer: Lee Ann McKevitt
Associate Managing Editor: Tracey Kuehn
Project Editor: Dana Kasowitz
Production Manager: Barbara Anne Seixas
Composition: Northeastern Graphic, Inc.
Printing and Binding: RR Donnelley

Library of Congress Control Number: 2010941506

ISBN-13: 978-1-4292-3344-6
ISBN-10: 1-4292-3344-3

© 2012, 2008, 2005, 2002 by Worth Publishers

Printed in the United States of America

First Printing 2011

Worth Publishers
41 Madison Avenue
New York, NY 10010
www.worthpublishers.com

Contents

Preface   vii

About the Author   ix

Introduction   1

part one
whiteness: the power of invisibility

1 The Matter of Whiteness–*Richard Dyer*   9

2 Failing to See–*Harlon Dalton*   15

3 Representations of Whiteness in the Black Imagination
  –*bell hooks*   19

Questions for Thinking, Writing, and Discussion for
Part One   25

part two
whiteness: the power of the past

1 The History of White People–*Nell Irvin Painter*   29

2 The Roots of Racial Classification–*Philip C. Wander, Judith
  N. Martin, and Thomas K. Nakayama*   33

3 How White People Became White–*James E. Barrett and
  David Roediger*   39

4 How Jews Became White Folks–*Karen Brodkin*   45

5 Becoming Hispanic: Mexican Americans and Whiteness
  –*Neil Foley*   59

6 The Possessive Investment in Whiteness
–George Lipsitz **71**

7 Global White Supremacy–*Charles W. Mills* **95**

Questions for Thinking, Writing, and Discussion for
Part Two **103**

part three
whiteness: the power of privilege

1 Making Systems of Privilege Visible–*Stephanie M. Wildman
with Adrienne D. Davis* **107**

2 Privilege as Paradox–*Allan G. Johnson* **115**

3 White Privilege: Unpacking the Invisible Knapsack
–Peggy McIntosh **121**

4 White Privilege/White Supremacy–*Robert Jensen* **127**

5 Membership Has Its Privileges: Thoughts on
Acknowledging and Challenging Whiteness
–Tim Wise **133**

6 People of Color Talk is Cheap–*Jusin Podur* **137**

Questions for Thinking, Writing, and Discussion for
Part Three **141**

part four
whiteness: the power of resistance

1 Breaking the Silence–*Beverly Tatum* **145**

2 Confronting One's Own Racism–*Joe Feagin and
Hernan Vera* **151**

3 How White People Can Serve as Allies to People of Color
in the Struggle to End Racism–*Paul Kivel* **157**

Questions for Thinking, Writing, and Discussion for
Part Four **167**

Suggestions for Further Reading **169**

Acknowledgments **172**

Index **174**

Preface

Like the earlier editions, this fourth edition brings together key essays and articles that seek to make whiteness visible so that we can analyze the nature of white privilege and use that knowledge to combat racism and related forms of inequality. It comes at a time when a surprising number of people claim that racism is a thing of the past. Many writers and commentators talk about the current period as a post-racial time but the statistics in this volume, along with the headlines in the daily papers and the TV news reports, tell a different story. While the appearance of racism has been muted, its impact and its hold on this nation have not changed significantly. That is why I believe that we must teach and talk about the many ways that privilege is built into our society and come to terms with why its manufactured invisibility is so effective and its consequences so lethal.

Like its predecessors, this new edition continues to include well-known essays and book excerpts from writers like Peggy McIntosh, Richard Dyer, bell hooks, Beverly Tatum, and George Lipsitz, as well as important contributions from Robert Jensen, Harlon Dalton, Time Wise, and many others. While retaining most, but not all, of the articles from the last edition, I have added three new pieces that I believe enrich or complicate our understanding of these issues. For example, in "The History of White People," Nell Irvin Painter firmly rejects the idea that race is a biological fact while acknowledging that many people continue to believe in this "superstition." This new edition replaces the article by Robert Jensen with a different selection by the same writer, one that updates and challenges some important statistics about the differences between white and racial/ethnic minorities, and the article by Justin Podur further complicates our discussion of language by examining the different ways that people use the phrase "people of color" and examines their implications, both negative and positive. In carrying out this revision, I have again avoided the temptation to lengthen the book significantly for fear that this would undermine rather than enhance its usefulness.

To all the faculty and students, too numerous to name, who have taken the time to contact me to tell me how much this book has meant to them and to share their stories, please know how much I appreciate and value your experience. To all the audiences I have spoken to and with in an ongoing effort to make sense out of whiteness and white privilege, please know how much I have learned from you and how much I appreciate your thoughtful engagement with this topic.

As with any book, this volume owes its existence to intentional and unintentional contributions on the part of many people. I am grateful to the many friends and neighbors in my town who care deeply about public education and who continue to demand equity and access for all our children and to the many people around the country who have come to hear me talk about privilege and who have shared with me their commitment to creating a more just and equitable society. The work of many scholars and educators has been very important to me, and many of them, though certainly not all, are represented in the list of suggestions for further reading that appears at the end of this volume. Finally, I am grateful to the people on the front lines who serve as allies in the struggle for a more just and equitable world.

My thanks to the talented people at Worth Publishers who take such good care of my books and who care deeply about the issues they seek to address. My editors Erik Gilg and Sarah Berger, designers Barbara Reingold and Kevin Kall, project editor Dana Kasowitz, production manager Barbara Seixas, and permissions manager Katrina Washington have all left their mark on this volume and it would not exist without them.

Finally, my thanks to my partner, Greg Mantsios, and our children, Alexi Mantsios and Andrea Mantsios, for endless uncompromising conversations about the nature of privilege and inequality as well as a lifetime of support.

About the Author

Paula Rothenberg writes, lectures, and consults on a variety of topics including multicultural curriculum transformation, issues of inequality, equity, and privilege, globalizing the curriculum, and white privilege. From 1989 to 2006, she served as Director of The New Jersey Project on Inclusive Scholarship, Curriculum, and Teaching, and Professor of Philosophy and Women's Studies at The William Paterson University of New Jersey. She is the author of *Invisible Privilege: A Memoir About Race, Class, and Gender,* (University Press of Kansas), and, with Worth Publishers, *Race, Class, and Gender,* Eighth Edition (2010), *Beyond Borders: Thinking Critically About Global Issues* (2006), and her newest book, *What's The Problem? A Brief Guide to Thinking Critically* (2010). Paula Rothenberg is also coeditor of a number of other anthologies, including *Creating an Inclusive College Curriculum: A Teaching Sourcebook from the New Jersey Project* and *Feminist Frameworks: Alternative Theoretical Accounts of the Relations Between Women and Men.* Her articles and essays appear in journals and anthologies across the disciplines and have been widely reprinted.

Central to the meaning of whiteness is a broad, collective American silence. The denial of white as a racial identity, the denial that whiteness has a history, allows the quiet, the blankness, to stand as the norm.

Grace Elizabeth Hale, *Making Whiteness:*
The Culture of Segregation in the South, 1890–1940

White people's lack of consciousness about their racial identities has grave consequences in that it not only denies white people the experience of seeing themselves as benefiting from racism, but in doing so, frees them from taking responsibility for eradicating it.

Alice McIntyre, *Making Meaning of Whiteness*

Given America's history, why should anyone be surprised to find white privilege so woven into the unexamined institutional practices, habits of mind, and received truths that Americans can barely see it?

Michael K. Brown et al., *Whitewashing Race*

Race is a social concept, not a scientific one.

Nell Irvin Painter, *The History of White People*

Introduction

Why talk about "whiteness" and white privilege? On the one hand, these topics make some people uncomfortable by seeming to take them to task for privileges they never noticed they had and, on the other, these topics appear to divert attention from racism and its effects, making white people the center of attention once again. But rather than providing reasons to avoid talking about whiteness and white privilege, these concerns actually underscore our need to do so. Discomfort of this kind is a sure sign that we need to continue the conversation. If education is about learning to see the world in new ways, it is bound, at times, to leave us feeling confused or angry or challenged. And this is a good thing. Instead of seeking to avoid such feelings, we should probably welcome a degree of discomfort in our lives and feel short-changed if it is not present.

As for the concern that looking at whiteness and white privilege will deflect our attention from racism, this could not be further from the truth. White privilege is the other side of racism. Unless we name it, we are in danger of wallowing in guilt or moral outrage with no idea of how to move beyond them. It is often easier to deplore racism and its effects than to take responsibility for the privileges some of us receive as a result of it. By choosing to look at white privilege, we gain an understanding of who benefits from racism, and how they do so. Once we understand how white privilege operates, we can begin to take steps to dismantle it on both a personal and an institutional level.

The project of interrogating whiteness and identifying white privilege will have a different meaning for us depending upon our own racial/ethnic background. While some of us who are white may be uncomfortable with the conversation and seek ways to deny responsibility for benefiting from white privilege, others may feel guilty and become overwhelmed with a sense of responsibility for enjoying an unearned advantage. Some of us who are not white may feel that we have long been aware of the power of whiteness to shape culture and values and may feel we have intimate knowledge of how white privilege operates. Others who are not white may feel a sense of confusion when confronted with the claim that whiteness provides the norm or standard by which most other things are judged. Wherever we are and whatever experiences, doubts, and expectations we bring to this project, we are likely to find that the very diversity of our backgrounds and the specific relationship we have to the questions being raised and studied will turn out to be important and valuable aspects of a shared learning experience. Whiteness and white privilege will look different and have different meanings for everyone reading these essays; by sharing our perspectives, each of us is likely to become aware of aspects of our society and forms of social interaction that previously were hidden from us.

The articles in Part One of this book are designed to help make whiteness visible. For the most part, these authors agree that whiteness has often gone unnamed and unexamined because it has been uncritically and unthinkingly adopted as the norm throughout society. When people of color are asked to reflect on their childhood and to try to remember when and how they learned about race, they usually have very specific memories of when and how they "discovered" or were taught that they were "African American," "Korean," "Caribbean," "Chinese," "Puerto Rican," "Latina," etc. The stories sometimes include painful memories of being invited to a classmate's home to play, only to find that the color of their skin suddenly made them unwelcome there. Or they involve memories of white dolls with yellow hair that looked nothing like them or incidents in the school playground or on the ball field where they were told in no uncertain terms that they did not belong. When whites are asked a similar question, they often draw a blank. Many cannot remember a time when they first "noticed" that they were white because whiteness was, for them, unremarkable. It was always everywhere. They learned to remark on "difference" by noticing who was not like them. From an early age, race, for white people, is about everyone else. While having black skin or almond-shaped eyes or coarse and curly hair are clearly signs of "difference" according to mainstream U.S. culture, having yellow hair or green eyes or white skin is often not viewed in this way by the people who possess them. That is because it is always whiteness that is centered and assumed. Difference is understood in relation to it. From this assumed but unnoticed perspective, white people are not "different" from, say, Native Americans; it is always the Native American (or other person of color) who is different. According to this unexamined point of view, to be white, as many authors have pointed out, is simply to be "human."

As Harlon Dalton and others have observed, this culturally encouraged invisibility has been an essential part of the power of whiteness. It has allowed some white people to create a world in their own image and a system of values that reinforces the power and privilege of those who are white people. At the same time, because of its invisibility, it has helped foster the illusion that those who succeed do so because of their superior intelligence, their hard work, or their determination, rather than, at least in part, their privilege. The power of whiteness is that it gives certain people an advantage without ever acknowledging that this is the case. Hence the title of Part One: "Whiteness: The Power of Invisibility."

Many recent books and articles have argued that whiteness is itself a social construct. By this they suggest that the very meaning of whiteness is part of an elaborately constructed mosaic of social and cultural meanings. Each of us is born with a particular collection of physical attributes, but it is society that teaches us which ones to value and which ones to reject. To suggest that whiteness is socially constructed is simply to notice that who counts as white and what it means to be white change over time and from place to place. For example, as several articles in Part Two point out, at one time in the not too distant past in the United States, Italians, Greeks, Jews, the Irish, and other "white" ethnic groups were not considered to be white. Over time and through an identifiable process described in these essays, the category of "white" was reshaped to include them. The changing meanings of whiteness and who was allowed to claim it are at the heart of the claim that whiteness is a social construct.

Like whiteness, white privilege has often been invisible to those who benefit from it most. The articles in Part Three go into great detail examining and enumerating the kinds of benefits that white people have received and continue to receive in U.S. society. Pointing to seemingly trivial, everyday, taken-for-granted privileges, such as the ability to go into a store and look at merchandise without being followed or viewed with suspicion, the privilege of never being asked to speak on behalf of all people in your racial group when you offer an opinion, and the right to drive about freely in suburban neighborhoods and on U.S. highways, or even in your own neighborhood, without worrying that the color of your skin will make you vulnerable to unwarranted harassment by law enforcers, these authors ask us to understand the power of white privilege.

Some of those of us who are white have a hard time accepting the idea that white privilege is a powerful force in society because we do not *feel* privileged. This is true because "white privilege" is not the same for all people with white-looking skin. Being white *and* wealthy usually brings with it more privileges and opportunities than simply having white skin— and looking white, having money, *and* being male compounds race and class privilege with gender or male privilege as well. For people whose class position or gender or both place them at a disadvantage, the deprivations and inequities imposed by class and/or male privilege may be so overwhelming that they mask the privileges some of us receive simply by virtue of being white. Other white people have a hard time accepting the idea of white privilege because they have been benefiting from it for so long that they can no longer distinguish between their privilege and their sense of who they are. People who are used to riding in the front of the bus and who have never ridden anywhere else don't think of their place on the bus as a privilege; for them, it is simply "the way things have always been." Because so much of their privilege is simply coextensive with their life, they do not notice their privilege any more than they notice their whiteness. This means that writers who seek to make both whiteness and the privileges it carries with it visible, face a difficult task. The articles in Part Three go to great lengths to specify the kinds of privileges that white people enjoy in this society, often quite apart from their intentions or their conscious choices.

But, let us assume that I am a white person, and after reading the articles in this book I am persuaded that there is such a thing as white privilege and that I benefit from it. Why might I want to rid myself of that privilege rather than continue to enjoy it and pass it along to my children? The answer has to do with simple notions of fairness and justice. Most people would feel little sense of pride or accomplishment in winning a race they started with an unfair advantage or winning a game when the deck was stacked in their favor. The satisfaction of such "victories" is short-lived at best. Once I begin to recognize how much of my success is a consequence of unfair advantage, I cannot help but begin to seek ways to make amends. This does not mean that I am not smart, nor does it mean that I have not worked hard—I have worked very hard in my life to accomplish my goals—but it does mean that I recognize that there are others equally smart who worked equally hard and who have a great deal less to show for it, simply because they are not white. Speaking very personally, this is a situation that I find intolerable. As a parent, I want the best for my children, but not at the expense of some other mother's child. As a person, I want to be successful and happy in my life, but my ability to enjoy my own success is limited when I realize that the racism from which I profit has destroyed the lives of many people of talent, even of genius.

Beyond questions of justice are matters of self-interest. History tells us that in the end, an unjust and inequitable distribution of resources and opportunities leads to terrible violence. Increasingly, wealthy white people in America find themselves living in gated communities as they seek ways to protect their lives and their property, and people of all racial/ethnic backgrounds and every economic class complain of feeling unsafe on the streets and in their homes. A society that distributes educational opportunities, housing, health care, food, even kindness, based on the color of people's skin and other arbitrary variables cannot guarantee the safety or security of its people. In this sense, all of us, both the victims and the beneficiaries of racism, pay a terrible price.

But if white people often benefit from their privilege quite apart from any deliberate decision to do so, what can those of us who are white and who do not wish to continue to make use of this unfair advantage over others do? The articles in Part Four provide the beginning of an answer to this question. Because white privilege is institutionalized in the United States, that is, because it is woven into the fabric of society, some might argue that it is virtually impossible for whites *not* to reap the benefits of this privilege. If this is true, then the challenge for those of us who are white is to find ways to use that privilege to combat racism and the system of privilege as a whole. If, for example, white privilege makes it easier for white people to get a hearing in some situations, then those of us who are white can use that opportunity to speak out against racism and other social inequities. We can protest incidents of racist harassment or intolerance on our campuses and challenge admissions policies that favor those who are white and well-to-do over those who are not. We can go to school board hearings and argue against public school budgets and policies that perpetuate white privilege. We can appear at town council meetings and speak out against zoning policies that perpetuate segregation while "protecting" white property values. We can speak out against racial profiling and police brutality. Closer to home, we can refuse to laugh at racist jokes and we can challenge our friends, neighbors, and colleagues when they, often thoughtlessly, parrot positions that reinforce the unfair advantages that white people enjoy in a myriad of venues. The first step toward dismantling the system of privilege that operates in this society is to name it and the second is for those of us who can to use our privileges to speak out against the system of privilege as a whole.

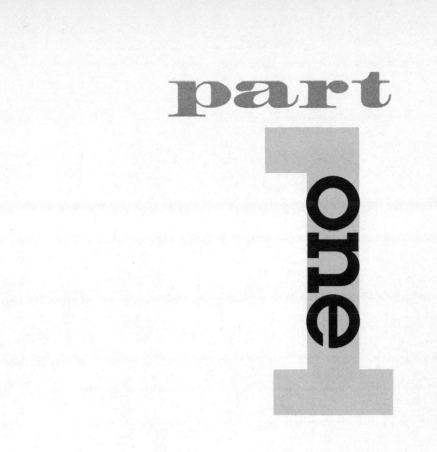

part 1 one

**whiteness:
the power of
invisibility**

The Matter of Whiteness

–Richard Dyer

Racial[1] imagery is central to the organisation of the modern world. At what cost regions and countries export their goods, whose voices are listened to at international gatherings, who bombs and who is bombed, who gets what jobs, housing, access to health care and education, what cultural activities are subsidised and sold, in what terms they are validated—these are all largely inextricable from racial imagery. The myriad minute decisions that constitute the practices of the world are at every point informed by judgments about people's capacities and worth, judgements based on what they look like, where they come from, how they speak, even what they eat, that is, racial judgements. Race is not the only factor governing these things and people of goodwill everywhere struggle to overcome the prejudices and barriers of race, but it is never not a factor, never not in play. And since race in itself—insofar as it is anything in itself—refers to some intrinsically insignificant geographical/physical differences between people, it is the imagery of race that is in play.

There has been an enormous amount of analysis of racial imagery in the past decades, ranging from studies of images of, say, blacks or American Indians in the media to the deconstruction of the fetish of the racial Other in the texts of colonialism and post-colonialism. Yet until recently a notable absence from such work has been the study of images of white people. Indeed, to say that one is interested in race has come to mean that one is interested in any racial imagery other than that of white people. Yet race is not only attributable to people who are not white, nor is imagery of non-white people the only racial imagery.

This essay is about the racial imagery of white people—not the images of other races in white cultural production, but the latter's imagery of white people themselves. This is not done merely to fill a gap in the analytic literature, but because there is something at stake in looking at, or continuing to ignore, white racial imagery. As long as race is something only applied to non-white peoples, as long as white people are not racially seen and named, they/we function as a human norm. Other people are raced, we are just people.

There is no more powerful position than that of being 'just' human. The claim to power is the claim to speak for the commonality of humanity. Raced people can't do that—they can only speak for their race.[2] But non-raced people can, for they do not represent the interests of a race. The point of seeing the racing of whites is to dislodge them/us from the position of power, with all the inequities, oppression, privileges and sufferings in its train, dislodging them/us by undercutting the authority with which they/we speak and act in and on the world.

The sense of whites as non-raced is most evident in the absence of reference to whiteness in the habitual speech and writing of white people in the West. We (whites) will speak of, say, the blackness or Chineseness of friends, neighbours, colleagues, customers or clients, and it may be in the most genuinely friendly and accepting manner, but we don't mention the whiteness of the white people we know. An old-style white comedian will often start a joke: 'There's this bloke walking down the street and he meets this black geezer', never thinking to race the bloke as well as the geezer. Synopses in listings of films on TV, where wordage is tight, none the less squander words with things like: 'Comedy in which a cop and his black sidekick investigate a robbery', 'Skinhead Johnny and his Asian lover Omar set up a laundrette', 'Feature film from a promising Native American director' and so on. Since all white people in the West do this all the time, it would be invidious to quote actual examples, and so I shall confine myself to one from my own writing. In an article on lesbian and gay stereotypes (Dyer 1993), I discuss the fact that there can be variations on a type such as the queen or dyke. In the illustrations which accompany this point, I compare a 'fashion queen' from the film *Irene* with a 'black queen' from *Car Wash*—the former, white image is not raced, whereas all the variation of the latter is reduced to his race. Moreover, this is the only non-white image referred to in the article, which does not however point out that all the other images discussed are white. In this, as in the other white examples in this paragraph, the fashion queen is, racially speaking, taken as being just human.

This assumption that white people are just people, which is not far off saying that whites are people whereas other colours are something else, is endemic to white culture. Some of the sharpest criticism of it has been aimed at those who would think themselves the least racist or white supremacist. bell hooks, for instance, has noted how amazed and angry white liberals become when attention is drawn to their whiteness, when they are seen by non-white people as white.

> Often their rage erupts because they believe that all ways of looking
> that highlight difference subvert the liberal belief in a universal

subjectivity (we are all just people) that they think will make racism disappear. They have a deep emotional investment in the myth of 'sameness', even as their actions reflect the primacy of whiteness as a sign informing who they are and how they think.

(hooks 1992: 167)

Similarly, Hazel Carby discusses the use of black texts in white classrooms, under the sign of multiculturalism, in a way that winds up focusing 'on the complexity of response in the (white) reader/student's construction of self in relation to a (black) perceived "other"'. We should, she argues, recognise that 'everyone in this social order has been constructed in our political imagination as a racialised subject' and thus that we should consider whiteness as well as blackness, in order 'to make visible what is rendered invisible when viewed as the normative state of existence: the (white) point in space from which we tend to identify difference' (Carby 1992: 193).

The invisibility of whiteness as a racial position in white (which is to say dominant) discourse is of a piece with its ubiquity. When I said above that I wasn't merely seeking to fill a gap in the analysis of racial imagery, I reproduced the idea that there is no discussion of white people. In fact for most of the time white people speak about nothing but white people, it's just that we couch it in terms of 'people' in general. Research—into books, museums, the press, advertising, films, television, software— repeatedly shows that in Western representation whites are overwhelmingly and disproportionately predominant, have the central and elaborated roles, and above all are placed as the norm, the ordinary, the standard.[3] Whites are everywhere in representation. Yet precisely because of this and their placing as norm they seem not to be represented to themselves *as* whites but as people who are variously gendered, classed, sexualised and abled. At the level of racial representation, in other words, whites are not of a certain race, they're just the human race.

We are often told that we are living now in a world of multiple identities, of hybridity, of decentredness and fragmentation. The old illusory unified identities of class, gender, race, sexuality are breaking up; someone may be black *and* gay *and* middle class *and* female; we may be bi-, poly- or non-sexual, of mixed race, indeterminate gender and heaven knows what class. Yet we have not yet reached a situation in which white people and white cultural agendas are no longer in the ascendant. The media, politics, education are still in the hands of white people, still speak for whites while claiming—and sometimes sincerely aiming—to speak for humanity. Against the flowering of a myriad postmodern voices, we must also see the countervailing tendency towards a homogenisation of world culture, in the continued dominance of US news dissemination, popular TV programmes and Hollywood movies. Postmodern multiculturalism may have genuinely opened up a space for the voices of the other, challenging the authority of the white West (cf. Owens 1983), but it may also simultaneously function as a side-show for white people who look on with delight at all the differences that surround them.[4] We may be on our way to genuine hybridity, multiplicity without (white) hegemony, and it may be where we want to get to — but we aren't there yet, and we won't get there until we see whiteness, see its power, its particularity and limitedness, put it in its place and end its rule. This is why studying whiteness matters.

It is studying whiteness *qua* whiteness. Attention is sometimes paid to 'white ethnicity' (e.g. Alba 1990), but this always means an identity based on cultural origins such as British, Italian or Polish, or Catholic or Jewish, or Polish American, Irish-American, Catholic-American and so on. These however are variations on white ethnicity (though some are more securely white than others), and the examination of them tends to lead away from a consideration of whiteness itself. John Ibson (1981), in a discussion of research on white US ethnicity, concludes that being, say, Polish, Catholic or Irish may not be as important to white Americans as some might wish. But being white is.

* * *

This then is why it is important to come to see whiteness. For those in power in the West, as long as whiteness is felt to be the human condition, then it alone both defines normality and fully inhabits it. As I suggested in my opening paragraphs, the equation of being white with being human secures a position of power. White people have power and believe that they think, feel and act like and for all people; white people, unable to see their particularity, cannot take account of other people's; white people create the dominant images of the world and don't quite see that they thus construct the world in their own image; white people set standards of humanity by which they are bound to succeed and others bound to fail. Most of this is not done deliberately and maliciously; there are enormous variations of power amongst white people, to do with class, gender and other factors; goodwill is not unheard of in white people's engagement with others. White power nonetheless reproduces itself regardless of in-tention, power differences and goodwill, and overwhelmingly because it is not seen as whiteness, but as normal. White people need to learn to see themselves as white, to see their particularity. In other words, whiteness needs to be made strange.

* * *

NOTES

1. I use the terms 'race' and 'racial' in this opening section in the most com-mon though problematic sense, referring to supposedly visibly differentiable, sup-posedly discrete social groupings.

2. In their discussion of the extraordinarily successful TV sitcom about a middle-class, African-American family, *The Cosby Show,* Sut Jhally and Justin Lewis note the way that viewers repeatedly recognise the characters' blackness but also feel that 'you just think of them as people'; in other words that they don't only speak for their race. Jhally and Lewis argue that this is achieved by the way the family conforms to 'the everyday, generic world of white television' (1992: 100), an essentially middle-class world. The family is 'ordinary' *despite* being black; because it is upwardly mobile, it can be accepted as 'ordinary', in a way that marginalises most actual African-Americans. If the realities of African-American experience were included, then the characters would not be perceived as 'just people'.

3. See, for instance, Bogle 1973, Hartmann and Husband 1974, Troyna 1981, MacDonald 1983, Wilson and Gutiérrez 1985, van Dijk 1987, Jhally and Lewis 1992 (58ff.), Ross 1995. The research findings are generally cast the other way round, in terms of non-white under-representation, textual marginalisation and positioning as deviant or a problem. Recent research in the US does suggest that African-Americans (but not other racially marginalised groups) have become more represented in the media, even in excess of their proportion of the population. However, this number still falls off if one focuses on central characters.

4. *The Crying Game* (GB 1992) seems to me to be an example of this. It explores, with fascination and generosity, the hybrid and fluid nature of identity: gender, race, national belonging, sexuality. Yet all of this revolves around a bemused but ultimately unchallenged straight white man—it reinscribes the position of those at the intersection of heterosexuality, maleness, and whiteness as that of the one group which does not need to be hybrid and fluid.

REFERENCES

Alba, Richard D. (1990) *Ethnic Identity: The Transformation of White America*, New Haven: Yale University Press.

Bogle, Donald (1973) *Toms, Coons, Mulattoes, Mammies and Bucks: An Interpretive History of Blacks in American Films*, New York: Viking Press.

Carby, Hazel V. (1992) 'The Multicultural Wars' in Dent, Gina (ed.) *Black Popular Culture*, Seattle: Bay Press, 187–99.

Dyer, Richard (1993) 'Seen To Be Believed: Problems in the Representation of Gay People as Typical' in Dyer *The Matter of Images: Essays on Representations*, London: Routledge, 19–51.

Hartmann, Paul and Husband, Charles (1974) *Racism and the Mass Media*, London: Davis-Poynter.

hooks, bell (1992) 'Madonna: Plantation Mistress or Soul Sister?' and 'Representations of Whiteness in the Black Imagination' in *Black Looks: Race and Representation*, Boston: South End Press, 157–64, 165–78.

Ibson, John (1981) 'Virgin Land or Virgin Mary? Studying the Ethnicity of White Americans', *American Quarterly* 33(3): 284–308.

Jhally, Sut and Lewis, Justin (1992) *Enlightened Racism: 'The Cosby Show', Audiences and the Myth of the American Dream*, Boulder: Westview Press.

MacDonald, J. F. (1983) *Blacks and White TV: Afro-Americans in Television since 1948*, Chicago: Nelson-Hall.

Owens, Craig (1983) 'The Discourse of Others: Feminists and Postmodernism' in Foster, Hal (ed.) *The Anti-Aesthetic: Essays on Postmodern Culture,* Port Townsend WA: Bay Press, 57–82.

Ross, Karen (1995) *Black and White Media,* Oxford: Polity.

Troyna, Barry (1981) 'Images of Race and Racist Images in the British News Media' in Halloran, J. D. (ed.) *Mass Media and Mass Communications,* Leicester: Leicester University Press.

van Dijk, T. A. (1987) *Communicating Racism,* London: Sage.

Wilson, C. J. and Gutiérrez, F. (1985) *Minorities and Media,* Beverley Hills: Sage.

Failing to See

–Harlon Dalton

Most White people, in my experience, tend not to think of themselves in racial terms. They know that they are White, of course, but mostly that translates into being not Black, not Asian-American, and not Native American. Whiteness, in and of itself, has little meaning.[1]

For a significant chunk, the inability to "get" race, and to understand why it figures so prominently in the lives of most people of color, stems from a deep affliction—the curse of rugged individualism. All of us, to some degree, suffer from this peculiarly American delusion that we are individuals first and foremost, captains of our own ships, solely responsible for our own fates. When taken to extremes, this ideal is antagonistic to the very idea of community. Even families cease to be vibrant social organisms; instead they are viewed as mere incubators and support systems for the individuals who happen to be born into them.

For those who embrace the rugged individualist ideal with a vengeance and who have no countervailing experience of community, the idea that a person's sense of self could be tied to that of a group is well-nigh incomprehensible. Collective concerns can only be interpreted as "groupthink"; collective responsibility as some strange foreign ideology. I frankly despair of being able to reach such people. Fortunately, most Americans, whatever their professed ideals, know from personal experience what community feels like. They are meaningfully connected to something smaller than the nation and larger than themselves.

For some, the tie is to a particular region of the country. I have a former colleague, for example, whose West Texas accent seemed to get stronger the longer he remained away from home. For others, the connection is to a religious community, or to a profession, or to a community defined by shared ideals or aspirations, such as Alcoholics Anonymous and the Benevolent and Protective Order of Elks. Perhaps most significantly,

15

many Americans eagerly lay claim to their ethnic heritage. It is, for them, a rich source of comfort, pride, and self-understanding. It provides shape and texture to their lives.

So-called White ethnics are not alone in this respect. Hyphenated Americans of all colors draw great strength from their ethnic roots, and take pride in those characteristics that make their ethnic group distinctive. Ethnicity is as significant a social force for Vietnamese-Americans living in Virginia and Chinese-Americans living in the borough of Queens as it is for Irish-Americans in South Boston and Polish-Americans in Chicago. Chicanos, Salvadorans, Puerto Ricans, and Cuban-Americans readily distinguish among one another even though their Anglo neighbors can't (or don't bother trying to) tell them apart. West Indians and U.S.-born African-Americans are as distinct from one another as steel drums are from saxophones. Lakota Sioux are not Navajo are not Pequot are not Crow.

On the other hand, from what I have observed, people who trace their ethnic roots to Europe tend to think quite differently about race than do people who hail from the rest of the world. Most non-White ethnics recognize that, at least in the American context, they have a race as well as an ethnicity. They understand full well that the quality of their lives is affected by these two social categories in distinct ways. White ethnics, on the other hand, are much less likely to think of themselves in racial terms. Like Whites who don't identify strongly with any ethnic group, they tend to take race for granted or to view it as somehow irrelevant.

At the same time, many White ethnics rely on their experience of ethnicity to draw conclusions about the operation of race in America. Drawing parallels makes sense to them because they regard White ethnicity and non-White race as being more or less equivalent. However, as the average Korean-American or Haitian immigrant can attest, despite their surface similarities, race and ethnicity are very different creatures.

Ethnicity is the bearer of culture. It describes that aspect of our heritage that provides us with a mother tongue and that shapes our values, our worldview, our family structure, our rituals, the foods we eat, our mating behavior, our music—in short, much of our daily lives. We embody our ethnicity without regard for the presence or absence of other ethnic groups. Of course, ethnic groups influence one another in myriad ways, and more than occasionally come into conflict. But they do not need each other to exist.

In contrast, races exist only in relation to one another. Whiteness is meaningless in the absence of Blackness; the same holds in reverse. Moreover, race itself would be meaningless if it were not a fault line along which power, prestige, and respect are distributed. Thus, during the war in Vietnam the North Vietnamese did not distinguish between Black Americans and White ones, since both seemed equally powerful with an M-16 in their hands. While ethnicity determines culture, race determines social position. Although the members of a given ethnic group may, for a time, find themselves on the bottom by virtue of their recent arrival, their lack of language or job skills, or even because of rank discrimination, that position usually is not long-term. *Race* and hierarchy, however, are indelibly wed.

Despite this distinction, much confusion is generated by the fact that for most American Blacks (excluding, for example, recent immigrants from the Caribbean), race and ethnicity are inextricably intertwined. The particulars of our African cultural heritage were largely, though not completely, destroyed by slavery. Part of what made the television miniseries *Roots* such a powerful experience for so many of us was that the protagonist was able to trace his heritage not only to a genetic African continent but to a particular country, particular village, and particular tribe. We long for that kind of deep-rootedness, but mostly we have to make do. From the remnants of our various African cultures, the rhythms of our daily existence, and the customs of our new home, especially the rural South and the urban inner city, we developed a uniquely African-American culture, with its own music, speech patterns, religious practices, and all the rest.

The emergence in the 1980s of the term "African-American" was meant to supply a label for our ethnicity that is distinct from the one used for race. Most people, however, continue to use the term "Black" to refer to both. "White," on the other hand, refers only to race. It has no particular cultural content. In ethnic terms, a random White person wandering through New York's Metropolitan Museum of Art could as easily be Irish-American, an immigrant from Greece, a Lithuanian transplant, or a Texan on vacation.

Why do most White people not see themselves as having a race? In part, race obliviousness is the natural consequence of being in the driver's seat. We are all much more likely to disregard attributes that seldom produce a ripple than we are those that subject us to discomfort. For example, a Reform Jewish family living in, say, Nacogdoches, Texas, will be more acutely aware of its religious/ethnic heritage than will the Baptist family next door. On the other hand, if that same family moved to the Upper West Side of Manhattan, its Jewishness would probably be worn more comfortably. For most Whites, race—or more precisely, their own race—is simply part of the unseen, unproblematic background.

Whatever the reason, the inability or unwillingness of many White people to think of themselves in racial terms has decidedly negative consequences. For one thing, it produces huge blind spots. It leaves them baffled by the amount of energy many Blacks pour into questions of racial identity. It makes it difficult for them to understand why many (but by no means all) Blacks have a sense of group consciousness that influences the choices they make as individuals. It blinds Whites to the fact that their lives are shaped by race just as much as are the lives of people of color. How they view life's possibilities; whom they regard as heroes; the extent to which they feel the country is theirs; the extent to which that belief is echoed back to them; all this and more is in part a function of their race.

This obliviousness also makes it difficult for many Whites to comprehend why Blacks interact with them on the basis of past dealings with other Whites, and why Blacks sometimes expect them to make up for the sins of their fathers, and of their neighbors as well. Curiously enough, many of the same folk wouldn't think twice about responding to young Black males as a type rather than as individuals.

Far and away the most troublesome consequence of race obliviousness is the failure of many to recognize the privileges our society confers on them because they have white skin.[2] White skin privilege is a birthright, a set of advantages one receives simply by being born with features that society values especially highly.

* * *

NOTES

1. Wellman, David T. (1993). *Portraits of White Racism*, 2d ed. Cambridge: Cambridge University Press, 194–95.
2. Ibid., 136–37, 163, 186–87.

chapter three 3

Representations of Whiteness in the Black Imagination

—bell hooks

Although there has never been any official body of black people in the United States who have gathered as anthropologists and/or ethnographers to study whiteness, black folks have, from slavery on, shared in conversations with one another "special" knowledge of whiteness gleaned from close scrutiny of white people. Deemed special because it was not a way of knowing that has been recorded fully in written material, its purpose was to help black folks cope and survive in a white supremacist society. For years, black domestic servants, working in white homes, acting as informants, brought knowledge back to segregated communities—details, facts, observations, and psychoanalytic readings of the white Other.

Sharing the fascination with difference that white people have collectively expressed openly (and at times vulgarly) as they have traveled around the world in pursuit of the Other and Otherness, black people, especially those living during the historical period of racial apartheid and legal segregation, have similarly maintained steadfast and ongoing curiosity about the "ghosts," "the barbarians," these strange apparitions they were forced to serve. . . .

I, too, am in search of the debris of history. I am wiping the dust off past conversations to remember some of what was shared in the old days when black folks had little intimate contact with whites, when we were much more open about the way we connected whiteness with the mysterious, the strange, and the terrible. Of course, everything has changed. Now many black people live in the "bush of ghosts" and do not know themselves separate from whiteness. They do not know this thing we call "difference." Systems of domination, imperialism, colonialism, and racism actively coerce black folks to internalize negative perceptions of blackness, to be self-hating. Many of us succumb to this. Yet, blacks who imitate

19

whites (adopting their values, speech, habits of being, etc.) continue to regard whiteness with suspicion, fear, and even hatred. This contradictory longing to possess the reality of the Other, even though that reality is one that wounds and negates, is expressive of the desire to understand the mystery, to know intimately through imitation, as though such knowing worn like an amulet, a mask, will ward away the evil, the terror.

Searching the critical work of post-colonial critics, I found much writing that bespeaks the continued fascination with the way white minds, particularly the colonial imperialist traveler, perceive blackness, and very little expressed interest in representations of whiteness in the black imagination. Black cultural and social critics allude to such representations in their writing, yet only a few have dared to make explicit those perceptions of whiteness that they think will discomfort or antagonize readers. James Baldwin's collection of essays, *Notes of a Native Son*, explores these issues with a clarity and frankness that is no longer fashionable in a world where evocations of pluralism and diversity act to obscure differences arbitrarily imposed and maintained by white racist domination. Addressing the way in which whiteness exists without knowledge of blackness even as it collectively asserts control, Baldwin links issues of recognition to the practice of imperialist racial domination. Writing about being the first black person to visit a Swiss village with only white inhabitants in his essay "Stranger in the Village," Baldwin notes his response to the village's yearly ritual of painting individuals black who were then positioned as slaves and bought so that the villagers could celebrate their concern with converting the souls of the "natives":

> I thought of white men arriving for the first time in an African village, strangers there, as I am a stranger here, and tried to imagine the astounded populace touching their hair and marveling at the color of their skin. But there is a great difference between being the first white man to be seen by Africans and being the first black man to be seen by whites. The white man takes the astonishment as tribute, for he arrives to conquer and to convert the natives, whose inferiority in relation to himself is not even to be questioned, whereas I, without a thought of conquest, find myself among a people whose culture controls me, has even, in a sense, created me, people who have cost me more in anguish and rage than they will ever know, who yet do not even know of my existence. The astonishment with which I might have greeted them, should they have stumbled into my African village a few hundred years ago, might have rejoiced their hearts. But the astonishment with which they greet me today can only poison mine.

My thinking about representations of whiteness in the black imagination has been stimulated by classroom discussions about the way in which the absence of recognition is a strategy that facilitates making a group the Other. In these classrooms there have been heated debates among students when white students respond with disbelief, shock, and rage, as they listen to black students talk about whiteness, when they are compelled to hear observations, stereotypes, etc., that are offered as "data" gleaned from close scrutiny and study. Usually, white students respond with naive amazement that black people critically assess white people from a standpoint where "whiteness" is the privileged signifier. Their amazement that black people watch white people with a critical "ethnographic" gaze is itself an expression of racism. Often their rage erupts because they believe that all ways of looking that highlight difference subvert the liberal belief in a universal subjectivity (we are all just people) that they think will make racism disappear. They have a deep emotional investment in the myth of "sameness," even as their actions reflect the primacy of whiteness as a sign informing who they are and how they think. Many of them are shocked that black people think critically about whiteness because racist thinking perpetuates the fantasy that the Other who is subjugated, who is subhuman, lacks the ability to comprehend, to understand, to see the working of the powerful. Even though the majority of these students politically consider themselves liberals and anti-racist, they too unwittingly invest in the sense of whiteness as mystery.

In white supremacist society, white people can "safely" imagine that they are invisible to black people since the power they have historically asserted, and even now collectively assert over black people, accorded them the right to control the black gaze. As fantastic as it may seem, racist white people find it easy to imagine that black people cannot see them if within their desire they do not want to be seen by the dark Other. One mark of oppression was that black folks were compelled to assume the mantle of invisibility, to erase all traces of their subjectivity during slavery and the long years of racial apartheid, so that they could be better, less threatening servants. An effective strategy of white supremacist terror and dehumanization during slavery centered around white control of the black gaze. Black slaves, and later manumitted servants, could be brutally punished for looking, for appearing to observe the whites they were serving, as only a subject can observe, or see. To be fully an object then was to lack the capacity to see or recognize reality. These looking relations were reinforced as whites cultivated the practice of denying the subjectivity of blacks (the better to dehumanize and oppress), of relegating them to the realm of the invisible. Growing up in a Kentucky household where black servants lived in the same dwelling with the white family who employed them, newspaper heiress Sallie Bingham recalls, in her autobiography *Passion and Prejudice*, "Blacks, I realized, were simply invisible to most white people, except as a pair of hands offering a drink on a silver tray." Reduced to the machinery of bodily physical labor, black people learned to appear before whites as though they were zombies, cultivating the habit of casting the gaze downward so as not to appear uppity. To look directly was an assertion of subjectivity, equality. Safety resided in the pretense of invisibility.

Even though legal racial apartheid no longer is a norm in the United States, the habits that uphold and maintain institutionalized white supremacy linger. Since most white people do not have to "see" black people (constantly appearing on billboards, television, movies, in magazines, etc.) and they do not need to be ever on guard nor to observe black people to be safe, they can live as though black people are invisible, and they can imagine that they are also invisible to blacks. Some white people may even imagine there is no representation of whiteness in the black imagination, especially one that is based on concrete observation or mythic conjecture. They think they are seen by black folks only as they want to appear. Ideologically, the rhetoric of white supremacy supplies a fantasy of whiteness. Described in Richard Dyer's essay "White," this fantasy makes whiteness synonymous with goodness:

> Power in contemporary society habitually passes itself off as embodied in the normal as opposed to the superior. This is common to all forms of power, but it works in a peculiarly seductive way with whiteness, because of the way it seems rooted, in common-sense thought, in things other than ethnic difference. . . . Thus it is said (even in liberal textbooks) that there are inevitable associations of white with light and therefore safety, and black with dark and therefore danger, and that this explains racism (whereas one might well argue about the safety of the cover of darkness, and the danger of exposure to the light); again, and with more justice, people point to the Jewish and Christian use of white and black to symbolize good and evil, as carried still in such expressions as "a black mark," "white magic," "to blacken the character" and so on. Socialized to believe the fantasy, that whiteness represents goodness and all that is benign and non-threatening, many white people assume this is the way black people conceptualize whiteness. They do not imagine that the way whiteness makes its presence felt in black life, most often as terrorizing imposition, a power that wounds, hurts, tortures, is a reality that disrupts the fantasy of whiteness as representing goodness.

. . . Looking past stereotypes to consider various representations of whiteness in the black imagination, I appeal to memory, to my earliest recollections of ways these issues were raised in black life. Returning to memories of growing up in the social circumstances created by racial apartheid, to all-black spaces on the edges of town, I reinhabit a location where black folks associated whiteness with the terrible, the terrifying, the terrorizing. White people were regarded as terrorists, especially those who dared to enter that segregated space of blackness. As a child, I did not know any white people. They were strangers, rarely seen in our neighborhoods. The "official" white men who came across the tracks were there to sell products, Bibles and insurance. They terrorized by economic exploitation. What did I see in the gazes of those white men who crossed our thresholds that made me afraid, that made black children unable to speak? Did they understand at all how strange their whiteness appeared in our living rooms, how threatening? Did they journey across the tracks with the same "adventurous" spirit that other white men carried to Africa, Asia, to those mysterious places they would one day call the "third world"? Did they come to our houses to meet the Other face-to-face and enact the colonizer role, dominating us on our own turf?

Their presence terrified me. Whatever their mission, they looked too much like the unofficial white men who came to enact rituals of terror and torture. As a child, I did not know how to tell them apart, how to ask the "real white people to please stand up."

*   *   *

In the absence of the reality of whiteness, I learned as a child that to be "safe," it was important to recognize the power of whiteness, even to fear it, and to avoid encounter. There was nothing terrifying about the sharing of this knowledge as survival strategy, the terror was made real only when I journeyed from the black side of town to a predominantly white area near my grandmother's house. I had to pass through this area to reach her place. Describing these journeys "across town" in the essay "Homeplace: A Site of Resistance," I remembered:

> It was a movement away from the segregated blackness of our community into a poor white neighborhood. I remember the fear, being scared to walk to Baba's, our grandmother's house, because we would have to pass that terrifying whiteness — those white faces on the porches staring us down with hate. Even when empty or vacant those porches seemed to say *danger,* you do not belong here, you are not safe.

Oh! that feeling of safety, of arrival, of homecoming when we finally reached the edges of her yard, when we could see the soot black face of our grandfather, Daddy Gus, sitting in his chair on the porch, smell his cigar, and rest on his lap. Such a contrast, that feeling of arrival, of homecoming — this sweetness and the bitterness of that journey, that constant reminder of white power and control. Even though it was a long time ago that I made this journey, associations of whiteness with terror and the terrorizing remain. Even though I live and move in spaces where I am surrounded by whiteness, there is no comfort that makes the terrorism disappear. All black people in the United States, irrespective of their class status or politics, live with the possibility that they will be terrorized by whiteness.

*   *   *

QUESTIONS FOR THINKING, WRITING, AND DISCUSSION FOR PART ONE

1. What does Richard Dyer mean when he says that "racial imagery is central to the organization of the modern world"? Do you agree or disagree? Argue for your answer by providing lots of specific examples to support your position.

2. Harlon Dalton suggests that most white people tend not to think of themselves in racial terms. What does he mean when he says this? Do you agree with him?

3. bell hooks writes: "In a white supremacist society, white people can 'safely' imagine that they are invisible to black people since the power they have historically asserted, and even now collectively assert over black people, accorded them the right to control the black gaze." What does it mean to have the right to control the black gaze? How does she elaborate on her claim?

4. All three writers in this section are concerned with what they call "the invisibility of whiteness." How can something be invisible if it's everywhere?

5. Why do the authors in this section believe it is important to study whiteness?

part two

2

whiteness: the power of the past

The History of White People
—*Nell Irvin Painter*

[Nell Irvin Painter begins her book by saying] I might have entitled this book *Constructions of White Americans from Antiquity to the Present,* because it explores a concept that lies within a history of events. I have chosen this strategy because race is an idea, not a fact, and its questions demand answers from the conceptual rather than the factual realm. American history offers up a large bounty of commentary on what it means to be nonwhite, moving easily between alternations in the meaning of race as color, from "colored" to "Negro" to "Afro-American" to "black" to "African American," always associating the idea of blackness with slavery. [1] But little attention has been paid to history's equally confused and flexible discourses on the white races and the old, old slave trade from eastern Europe.

I use "white races" in the plural, because for most of the past centuries—when race really came down to matters of law—educated Americans firmly believed in the existence of more than one European race. It is possible, and important, to investigate that other side of history without trivializing the history we already know so well.

Let me state categorically that while this is not history in white versus black, I do not by any means underestimate or ignore the overwhelming importance of black race in America. I am familiar with the truly gigantic literature that explains the meaning, importance, and honest-to-god reality of the existence of race when it means black. In comparison with this preoccupation, statutory and biological definitions of white race remain notoriously vague—the leavings of what is not black. But this vagueness does not indicate lack of interest—quite to the contrary, for another vast historical literature, much less known today, explains the meaning, importance, and honest-to-god reality of the existence of white races.

It may seem odd to begin a book on Americans in antiquity, a period long before Europeans discovered the Western Hemisphere and thousands of years before the invention of the concept of race. But given the prevalence of the notion that race is permanent, many believe it possible to trace something recognizable as the white race back more than two thousand years. In addition, not a few Westerners have attempted to racialize antiquity, making ancient history into white race history and classics into a lily-white field complete with pictures of blond ancient Greeks. Transforming the ancients into Anglo-Saxon ancestors made classics unwelcoming to African American classicists. [2] The blond-ancient-Greek narrative may no longer be taught in schools, but it lives on as a myth to be confronted in these pages.

Today we think of race as a matter of biology, but a second thought reminds us that the meanings of race quickly spill out of merely physical categories. Even in so circumscribed a place as one book, the meanings of white race reach into concepts of labor, gender, and class and images of personal beauty that seldom appear in analyses of race. Work plays a central part in race talk, because the people who do the work are likely to be figured as inherently deserving the toil and poverty of laboring status. It is still assumed, wrongly, that slavery anywhere in the world must rest on a foundation of racial difference. Time and again, the better classes have concluded that those people deserve their lot; it must be something within them that puts them at the bottom. In modern times, we recognize this kind of reasoning as it relates to black race, but in other times the same logic was applied to people who were white, especially when they were impoverished immigrants seeking work.

Those at the very bottom were slaves. Slavery has helped construct concepts of white race in two contradictory ways. First, American tradition equates whiteness with freedom while consigning blackness to slavery. The history of unfree white people slumbers in popular forgetfulness, though white slavery (like black slavery) moved people around and mixed up human genes on a massive scale. [3] The important demographic role of the various slave trades is all too often overlooked as a historical force. In the second place, the term "Caucasian" as a designation for white people originates in concepts of beauty related to the white slave trade from eastern Europe, and whiteness remains embedded in visions of beauty found in art history and popular culture.

Today most Americans envision whiteness as racially indivisible, though ethnically divided; this is the scheme anthropologists laid out in the mid-twentieth century. By this reckoning, there were only three real races ("Mongoloid," "Negroid," and "Caucasoid") but countless ethnicities. Today, however, biologists and geneticists (not to mention literary critics) no longer believe in the physical existence of races—though they recognize the continuing power of racism (the belief that races exist, and that some are better than others). It took some two centuries to reach this conclusion, after countless racial schemes had spun out countless different numbers of races, even of white races, and attempts at classification produced frustration.

Although science today denies race any standing as objective truth, and the U.S. census faces taxonomic meltdown, many Americans cling to race as the unschooled cling to superstition. So long as racial discrimination remains a fact of life and statistics can be arranged to support racial difference, the American belief in races will endure. But confronted with the actually existing American population—its distribution of wealth, power, and beauty—the notion of American whiteness will continue to evolve, as it has since the creation of the American Republic.

NOTES

1. We usually assume definitions of race as color to be straightforward, as though "black" Americans were always dark-skinned. But the long American history of racial adjudication—of deciding who counted legally as black and white—belies any strong equivalence between race as color and actual color of skin.

2. William Sanders Scarborough (1852–1926) was a founder of the American Philological Association, which asked him not to attend meetings after 1909.

3. Although Arthur de Gobineau's racial reasoning in *Essay on the Inequality of the Races* was wrongheaded in the extreme, he did grasp one fact of human history: economic development leads to demographic mixing, as the demand for labor draws in people from afar.

chapter two 2

The Roots of Racial Classification
–Philip C. Wander, Judith N. Martin,
and Thomas K. Nakayama

Skin color (whiteness, blackness, yellowness, etc.) remains a concern in the late 20th century, not because it advances the mission of multiculturalism, helps us to understand different people, or allows us, as individuals, to congratulate ourselves on our "color blindness," but because skin color has been used to rank order people for practical things like jobs, promotions, loans, and housing (Condit & Lucaites, 1993). The social significance of color also reveals itself in our poverty statistics. In 1986, the Catholic Bishops of the United States issued a report titled *Economic Justice and the U.S. Economy.* Harsh poverty, they observed, plagues our country despite its great wealth. Thirty-three million Americans are poor and another 20 to 30 million are needy. This problem, however, does not fall evenly on the population:

> These burdens fall most heavily on blacks, Hispanics and native Americans. Even more disturbing is the large increase in the number of women and children living in poverty. Today children are the largest single group among the poor. This tragic fact seriously threatens the nation's future. That so many people are poor in a nation as rich as ours is a social and moral scandal that we cannot ignore. (Catholic Bishops, 1991, p. 579)

Nearly 10 years later the statistics have, if anything, gotten worse. "Whiteness" does not stand alone. It draws part of its meaning from what it means to be nonwhite.

How did the concept of "whiteness" develop historically? How does it function in both the historical and contemporary United States? This seems to be a moment in the United States to take a new approach to discussions of race, identity, and communication. Our goal is to provide a *sociohistorical* basis for discussions of race that allows us to contextualize thought and behavior and move beyond discussions of individual racism.

. . . Whiteness refers to a *historical systemic structural* race-based superiority. Using the construct of whiteness allows a discussion where no *one* is a racist and permits an exploration of ways in which some people happily if unwittingly benefit from and informally reproduce patterns established by racism. Throughout this discussion, we emphasize that whiteness, like other categories, is "leaky"; that is, race can *only* be seen in relation to other categories, such as class, gender, sexuality, and so on, that render any category problematic.

RACIAL CATEGORIES IN THE NINETEENTH CENTURY

The roots of racial classification emerge from the naturalistic science of the 18th and 19th centuries. During this time, scientific studies extended the classifications of humankind developed by zoologists and physical anthropologists by systematically measuring and describing differences in hair texture, skin color, average height, and cranial capacity in various races. These studies reflected a naturalist tradition—an assumption that the physical world had an intrinsically hierarchical order in which whites were the last and most developed link in "the great chain of being" (Webster, 1992, p. 4). . . .

How were these categories used socially and politically? To answer these questions, we must examine the historical contexts in which this scholarship occurred. This scholarship occurred during a period of global expansion by European powers and of westward expansion in the United States. The research on racial categories supported these efforts—often aimed at subjugating nonwhite peoples (Foner & Rosenberg, 1993; Omi & Winant, 1994).

Anthropologists and Egyptologists found evidence of cultural, social, technological, and spiritual inferiority of nonwhite races throughout human history. These conclusions were corroborated by colonial officials and newspaper reports that described and discussed the inferiority of nonwhites in colonies and potential colonies throughout the world.

FROM RACIAL CLASSIFICATION TO RACE THEORY

By using the research findings described above, race theory helped to explain and justify the expansion and colonizing by white peoples, their subjugation of nonwhite peoples in Africa, Asia, and the Orient, and the continuing domination of nonwhite peoples—slaves, peasants, aborigines, and the poor at home.

This attitude was also promoted by religious institutions. Presidents, scholars, theologians, and the elites in Europe and the United States in the 19th century proclaimed that the mission of the white race was to "civilize and Christianize" the heathen, the savages, the less fortunate—all lesser beings in God's creation. Defenders of slavery and colonialism claimed that these efforts were in fact a blessing to Africans—who by their biological inferiority were incapable of taking the first steps to civilization. This civilizing mission often included armed intervention and the establishment of empires, like Great Britain, that stretched around the world (Webster, 1992).

There was often fierce resistance. Colonial slaughter took the lives of tens of millions of people, six million in the Belgian Congo alone. There are many accounts of slave resistance in the United States, and there were white men and women who fought against white supremacy in the United States, in spite of the obvious benefits this supremacy afforded them (Aptheker, 1992; Chaudhuri & Strobel, 1992).

At first there were white and black slaves who suffered alike from the overwhelming English and European passion for material and spiritual expansion. A closer look at U.S. colonial history reveals the move from racial classification to racialization—as *slave* and *black* become synonymous. According to some scholars, this move was due to two unique characteristics of the American colonial experience. The first was the prevailing attitude toward property. For centuries, Europeans held a firm belief that the best in life was the expansion of self through property and property began and ended with possession of one's body (Kovel, 1984, p. 18). However, this law was violated by New World slavery, and it differed in this way from other slave systems. The slave owners, in proclaiming ownership of the bodies of slaves, detached the body from the self and then reduced this self to subhuman status (justified by the racial categorization system). Slave property became totally identified with people who happened to have black skin, the color that had always horrified the West (Kovel, 1984, p. 21).

The second characteristic revolves around the institutionalizing of slavery in the formation of the nation. There was some antislavery activity around the time of the War for Independence, but when the time came to structure the nation, the interests of property asserted themselves and the slave-race complex became part of the American culture and was made official in the Constitution where black slaves were quantified as three-fifths of a person for purposes of representation. Thus, the paradox of U.S. history: that the ideal of freedom is historically rooted in the institution of slavery and the two inextricably racialized (Morgan, 1975).

You might think that because skin color was so central to the law, that "whiteness" and "blackness" were carefully defined and easy to understand. They were defined by law, but they were not easy to understand in practice. The best minds in the Old South tried valiantly over the years to draw a legal line to define who was white and who was black, in order to maintain a racial hierarchy. The inferior were, by God's will, destined to be enslaved by the superior. Such was the happy blend of theology and race theory advanced by spokespersons for the master class (Wander, 1972).

But not all black people were slaves. There were free black people, even in the South. Some of them prospered and even owned slaves. On the slave plantations in the 19th century, there were dark-skinned slaves and there were slaves who were lighter-skinned than their "white" masters. Antebellum newspapers in the South sometimes carried stories about "white" children almost sold at auction.

Most white people in the Old South did not own slaves. Slave owners were a small but extremely powerful minority. When agitating for secession from the United States, they faced opposition from white farmers and workers who did not own slaves and did not idealize slavery as a way of organizing working-class people. Counties in Northern Alabama, a hilly country populated by white farmers and unsuitable for plantation agriculture, voted against secession.

Some members of the master class had reservations about slavery. The diaries of the wives of plantation owners at times reflect an awareness of their own condition as the property of males in their family who had complete control over their money and property. Some of these women expressed misgivings about the way their sons and husbands were "using" female slaves. Others expressed anger over how this "property" was misleading their husbands and sons.

There were white Southerners who objected to slavery. There were white Northerners who opposed its abolition. In the South, PSWMs (propertied, straight, white males) tended to defend slavery, especially those who held property in slaves; in the North, PSWMs tended to oppose or refuse to take a stand on abolition. In part, this related to interests linking wealthy people together, as in the case of the production of cotton in the South and its purchase by mill owners in the North, but it also related, in part, to the nature of the Abolitionist movement.

Abolitionism was the first mass-based movement in this country. It included blacks and whites, men and women, religious and nonreligious people. Those outside this movement sometimes found this alarming. Along with condemning slavery, abolitionists condemned the idea that working-class people, black or white, should be treated as slaves (a view advanced by the upper class in the South who argued that chattel slaves in the South were better off than "wage" slaves in the North). They also denounced a system in which women, black or white, were treated as property by men (Fuller, 1855/1971). Abolitionists not only wanted to abolish slavery, they wanted to abolish other forms of involuntary servitude as well, and this had implications for relations between the North and the South (Aptheker, 1989).

White abolitionists opposed slavery and sometimes worked with black people in the process, but they did not necessarily believe in racial equality. In part, among the abolitionists, were a society of people ("colonizationists") dedicated to sending black people back to Africa (Wander, 1971). When Frederick Douglass, a leading abolitionist, spoke to white and black audiences, white people sometimes came up afterward and touched his cheek. They could not believe a black man could be so brilliant an orator. They thought he might have bootblack on his face. Abraham Lincoln was a colonizationist. He believed in the racial superiority of white people, though he thought black people ought to be paid a fair day's wage for a fair day's work. People in the South thought he was an abolitionist in disguise. Abolitionists thought he was wishy-washy.

The above hints at the complexity of thinking about "whiteness" (and "blackness") in U.S. history. The confusion and the horror surrounding these complexities emerged, after the Civil War, in Jim Crow laws designed to keep the "races" apart. The law, pressured by the leaky nature of racial categories, devised a "one drop" theory—if you had one drop of "nonwhite blood" in your veins, you could not qualify as white. Not qualifying as white had, as the history of slavery and the exploitation of Indians shows (Frickey, 1993), tremendous implications for the ways people lived and even for their right to earn a living. Throughout our history, "whiteness" has, legally speaking, been a form of property (Harris, 1993).

At the turn of the 20th century, whites in the United States were pursuing the industrial, capitalist dream and a continued manifest destiny. As immigrants poured in to the United States to help with the expansion, however, nativism, anti-immigrant feelings (e.g., The Chinese Exclusion Act) ensured that the prosperity benefited mainly the whites. Poor European immigrants and the many Southern ex-slaves represented a potential massive threat to the existing powers. The answer was racism.

For example, in 1912, Woodrow Wilson proclaimed his wish that "justice be done to the colored people in every matter; and not mere grudging justice, but justice executed with liberality and cordial good feeling." He also, at the same time, issued an executive order that racially segregated eating and toilet facilities of federal civil service workers. The order also gave Southern federal officials the right to discharge or downgrade any black employee on any ground they saw fit. When a group of black leaders protested to the President, they were summarily dismissed (Kovel, 1984, p. 31).

As many scholars have noted, it is in the story of U.S. labor history in the first part of the 20th century that the racialization became solidified. W.E.B. DuBois (1935) describes how white laborers were paid meager monetary wages, but were provided additional public and psychological "wages": better schools and access to public facilities, deference, and so on. In continuing the story, Roediger (1991) shows how this category of whiteness was carefully constructed through trial and error to assure white workers a secure place in the sometimes fragile economy. The whites distanced themselves from blacks, projecting on to them qualities they themselves lacked—sensuality and spontaneity—and in stressing this contrast, allowed despised ethnic groups (Irish, Eastern Europeans, Jews) a way to transcend their minority status and assimilate into the majority (Roediger, 1991).

REFERENCES

Aptheker, H. (1989). *Abolitionism: A revolutionary movement.* Boston, MA: Twayne.

Aptheker, H. (1992). *Anti-racism in U.S. history: The first two hundred years.* New York: Greenwood.

Catholic Bishops of the United States. (1991). The idea of social justice. In J. Skolnick & E. Currie (Eds.), *Crisis in American institutions* (8th ed.; pp. 579–590). New York: Harper-Collins.

Chaudhuri, N., & Strobel, M. (Eds.). (1992). *Western women and imperialism.* Bloomington: Indiana University Press.

Condit, C., & Lucaites, J. (1993). *Crafting equality: America's Anglo-African world.* Chicago: University of Chicago Press.

DuBois, W. E. B. (1935). *Black reconstruction in America.* New York: Atheneum.

Foner, P., & Rosenberg, D. (Eds.). (1993). *Racism, dissent, and Asian Americans from 1850 to the present: A documentary history.* Westport, CT: Greenwood.

Frickey, P. P. (1993). Marshalling past and present: Colonialism, constitutionalism, and interpretation in Federal Indian Law. *Harvard Law Review, 107,* 381–440.

Fuller, M. (1971). *Woman in the nineteenth century.* New York: Norton. (Original work published 1855)

Harris, C. I. (1993). Whiteness as property. *Harvard Law Review, 106,* 1709–1791.

Kovel, J. (1984). *White racism: A psychohistory.* New York: Columbia University Press.

Morgan, E. (1975). *American slavery, American freedom: The ordeal of colonial Virginia.* New York: Norton.

Omi, M., & Winant, H. (1994). *Racial formation in the United States from the 1960s to the 1990s.* New York: Routledge.

Roediger, D. (1991). *The wages of whiteness: Race and the making of the American working class.* New York: Verso.

Wander, P. C. (1971). Salvation through separation: The image of the Negro in the American colonization society. *Quarterly Journal of Speech, 57,* 57–67.

Wander, P. C. (1972). The savage child: The image of the Negro in the pro-slavery movement. *Southern Speech Communication Journal, 57,* 335–360.

Webster, Y. (1992). *The racialization of American.* New York: St. Martin's.

How White People Became White
–James E. Barrett and David Roediger

> *By the eastern European immigration the labor force has been cleft horizontally into two great divisions. The upper stratum includes what is known in mill parlance as the English-speaking men; the lower contains the "Hunkies" or "Ginnies." Or, if you prefer, the former are the "white men," the latter the "foreigners."*
>
> **John Fitch,** *The Steel Workers*

In 1980, Joseph Loguidice, an elderly Italian-American from Chicago, sat down to give his life story to an interviewer. His first and most vivid childhood recollection was of a race riot that had occurred on the city's near north side. Wagons full of policemen with "peculiar hats" streamed into his neighborhood. But the "one thing that stood out in my mind," Loguidice remembered after six decades, was "a man running down the middle of the street hollering . . . 'I'm White, I'm White!'" After first taking him for an African-American, Loguidice soon realized that the man was a white coal handler covered in dust. He was screaming for his life, fearing that "people would shoot him down." He had, Loguidice concluded, "got caught up in . . . this racial thing."[1]

Joseph Loguidice's tale might be taken as a metaphor for the situation of millions of "new immigrants" from Eastern and Southern Europe who arrived in the United States between the end of the nineteenth century and the early 1920s. That this episode made such a profound impression is in itself significant, suggesting both that this was a strange, new situation and that thinking about race became an important part of the consciousness of immigrants like Loguidice. How did this racial awareness and increasingly racialized worldview develop among new immigrant workers? Most did not arrive with conventional U.S. attitudes regarding "racial" difference, let alone its significance and implications in industrial America. Yet most, it seems, "got caught up in . . . this racial thing." How did this happen? If race was indeed socially constructed, then what was the raw material that went into the process?

How did these immigrant workers come to be viewed in racial terms by others— employers, the state, reformers, and other workers? Like the coal handler in Loguidice's story, their own ascribed racial identity was not always clear. A whole range of evidence—laws, court cases, formal racial ideology, social conventions, and popular culture in the form of slang, songs, films, cartoons, ethnic jokes, and popular theatre—suggests that the native born and older immigrants often placed the new immigrants not only *above* African- and Asian-Americans, for example, but also *below* "white" people. Indeed, many of the older immigrants, and particularly the Irish, had themselves been perceived as "nonwhite" just a generation earlier. As labor historians, we are interested in the ways in which Polish, Italian, and other European artisans and peasants became American workers, but we are equally concerned with the process by which they became "white." Indeed, in the U.S. the two identities merged, and this explains a great deal of the persistent divisions within the working-class population. How did immigrant workers wind up "inbetween"? . . .

We make no brief for the consistency with which "race" was used, by experts or popularly, to describe the "new immigrant" Southern and East Europeans who dominated the ranks of those coming to the U.S. between 1895 and 1924 and who "remade" the American working class in that period. We regard such inconsistency as important evidence of the "inbetween"[2] racial status of such immigrants. The story of Americanization is vital and compelling, but it took place in a nation also obsessed by race. For new immigrant workers the processes of "becoming white" and "becoming American" were connected at every turn. The "American standard of living," which labor organizers alternately and simultaneously accused new immigrants of undermining and encouraged them to defend via class organization, rested on "white men's wages." Political debate turned on whether new immigrants were fit to join the American nation and "American race." Nor do we argue that new immigrants from Eastern and Southern Europe were in the same situation as non-whites. Stark differences between the racialized status of African-Americans and the racial inbetween-ness of new immigrants meant that the latter *eventually* "became ethnic" and that their trajectory was predictable. But their history was sloppier than their trajectory. From day to day they were, to borrow from E. P. Thompson, "proto-nothing," reacting and acting in a highly racialized nation.[3]

America's racial vocabulary had no agency of its own, but rather reflected material conditions and power relations—the situations that workers faced on a daily basis in their workplaces and communities. Yet the words themselves were important. They were not only the means by which native born and elite people marked new immigrants as inferiors, but also those by which immigrant workers came to locate themselves and those about them in the nation's racial hierarchy. In beginning to analyze the vocabulary of race, it makes little sense for historians to invest the words themselves with an agency that could be exercised only by real historical actors, or meanings that derived only from the particular historical contexts in which the language was developed and employed.

The word *guinea,* for example, had long referred to African slaves, particularly those from the continent's northwest coast, and to their descendants. But from the late 1890s, the term was increasingly applied to southern European migrants, first and especially to Sicilians and southern Italians, who often came as contract laborers. At various times and places in the United States, *guinea* has been applied to mark Greeks, Jews, Portuguese, Puerto Ricans, and perhaps any new immigrant.[4]

Likewise, *hunky,* which began life, probably in the early twentieth century, as a corruption of "Hungarian," eventually became a pan-Slavic slur connected with perceived immigrant racial characteristics. By World War I the term was frequently used to describe any immigrant steelworker, as in *mill hunky.* Opponents of the Great 1919 Steel Strike, including some native born skilled workers, derided the struggle as a "hunky strike." Yet Josef Barton's work suggests that for Poles, Croats, Slovenians, and other immigrants who often worked together in difficult, dangerous situations, the term embraced a remarkable, if fragile, sense of prideful identity across ethnic lines. In *Out of This Furnace,* his epic novel of 1941 based on the lives of Slavic steelworkers, Thomas Bell observed that the word *hunky* bespoke "unconcealed racial prejudice" and a "denial of social and racial equality." Yet as these workers built the industrial unions of the late 1930s and took greater control over their own lives, the meaning of the term began to change. The pride with which second- and third-generation Slavic-American steelworkers, women as well as men, wore the label in the early 1970s seemed to have far more to do with class than with ethnic identity. At about the same time, the word *honky,* possibly a corruption of *hunky,* came into common use as black nationalism reemerged as a major ideological force in the African-American community.[5]

Words and phrases employed by social scientists to capture the inbetween identity of the new immigrants are a bit more descriptive, if more cumbersome. As late as 1937, John Dollard wrote repeatedly of the immigrant working class as "our temporary Negroes." More precise, if less dramatic, is the designation "not-yet-white ethnics" offered by immigration historian John Bukowczyk. The term not only reflects the popular perceptions and everyday experiences of such workers, but also conveys the dynamic quality of racial formation.[6]

The examples of Greeks and Italians particularly underscore the new immigrants' ambiguous positions with regard to popular perceptions of race. When Greeks suffered as victims of an Omaha race riot in 1909 and when eleven Italians died at the hands of lynchers in Louisiana in 1891, their less-than-white racial status mattered alongside their nationalities. Indeed, as Loguidice's coal handler shows, their ambivalent racial status put their lives in jeopardy. According to Gunther Peck's fine study of copper miners in Bingham, Utah, the Greek and Italian immigrants were "nonwhite" before their tension-fraught cooperation with the Western Federation of Miners during a 1912 strike ensured that "the category of Caucasian worker changed and expanded." Indeed, the work of Dan Georgakas and Yvette Huginnie shows that Greeks and other Southern Europeans often "bivouacked" with other "nonwhite" workers in Western mining towns. Pocatello, Idaho, Jim-Crowed Greeks in the early twentieth century and in Arizona they were not welcomed by white workers in "white men's towns" or "white men's jobs." In Chicago during the Great Depression, a German-American wife expressed regret over marrying her "half-nigger," Greek-American husband. African-American slang in the 1920s in South Carolina counted those of mixed American Indian, African-American, and white heritage as *Greeks*. Greek-Americans in the Midwest showed great anxieties about race, and were perceived not only as Puerto Rican, mulatto, Mexican, or Arab, but also as non-white *because of* being Greek.[7]

Italians, involved in a spectacular international diaspora in the early twentieth century, were racialized as the "Chinese of Europe" in many lands.[8] But in the U.S. their racialization was pronounced and, as *guinea's* evolution suggests, more likely to connect Italians with Africans. During the debate at the Louisiana state constitutional convention of 1898 over how to disfranchise blacks, and over which whites might lose the vote, some acknowledged that the Italian's skin "happens to be white" even as they argued for his disfranchisement. But others held that "according to the spirit of our meaning when we speak of 'white man's government,' [the Italians] are as black as the blackest negro in existence."[9] More than metaphor intruded on this judgment. At the turn of the century, a West Coast construction boss was asked, "You don't call the Italian a white man?" The negative reply assured the questioner that the Italian was "a dago." Recent studies of Italian- and Greek-Americans make a strong case that racial, not just ethnic, oppression long plagued "non-white" immigrants from Southern Europe.[10]

The racialization of East Europeans was likewise striking. While racist jokes mocked the black servant who thought her child, fathered by a Chinese man, would be a Jew, racist folklore held that Jews, inside-out, were "niggers." In 1926 Serbo-Croatians ranked near the bottom of a list of forty "ethnic" groups whom "white American" respondents were asked to order according to the respondents' willingness to associate with members of each group. They placed just above Negroes, Filipinos, and Japanese. Just above them were Poles, who were near the middle of the list. One sociologist has recently written that "a good many groups on this color continuum [were] not considered white by a large number of Americans."[11] The literal inbetween-ness of new immigrants on such a list suggests what popular speech affirms: The state of whiteness was approached gradually and controversially. The authority of the state itself both smoothed and complicated that approach.

NOTES

1. The epigraph is from John A. Fitch, *The Steel Workers* (New York, 1910), 147. Joe Sauris, Interview with Joseph Loguidice, July 25, 1980, Italians in Chicago Project, copy of transcript, Box 6, Immigration History Research Center, University of Minnesota, St. Paul, Minn.

2. We borrow "inbetween" from Robert Orsi, "The Religious Boundaries of an Inbetween People: Street Feste and the Problem of the Dark-Skinned 'Other' in Italian Harlem, 1920–1990," *American Quarterly,* 44 (September 1992): passim, and also from John Higham, *Strangers in the Land: Patterns of American Nativism, 1860–1925* (New York, 1974), 169.

3. Lawrence Glickman, "Inventing the 'American Standard of Living': Gender, Race and Working-Class Identity, 1880–1925," *Labor History,* 34 (Spring–Summer, 1993): 221–35; David Montgomery, *Beyond Equality: Labor and the Radical Republicans, 1862–1872* (Urbana, Ill., 1981), 254.

4. On *guinea*'s history, see David Roediger, "Guineas, Wiggers and the Dramas of Racialized Culture," *American Literary History,* 7 (1995): 654. On post-1890 usages, see William Harlen Gilbert, Jr., "Memorandum Concerning the Characteristics of the Larger Mixed-Blood Islands of the United States," *Social Forces,* 24 (March 1946): 442; *Oxford English Dictionary,* 2d ed. (Oxford, 1989), 6:937–38; Frederic G. Cassidy and Joan Houston Hall, eds., *Dictionary of American Regional English* (Cambridge and London, 1991), 2: 838.

5. Tamony's notes on *hunky* (or *hunkie*) speculate on links to *honky* (or *honkie*) and refer to the former as an "old labour term." By no means did *Hun* refer unambiguously to Germans before World War I. See, e.g., Henry White, "Immigration Restriction as a Necessity," *American Federationist,* 4 (June 1897): 67; Paul Krause, *The Battle for Homestead, 1880–1892: Politics, Culture and Steel* (Pittsburgh, 1992), 216–17; David Brody, *Steelworkers in America* (New York, 1969), 120–21. See also the *Mill Hunky Herald,* published in Pittsburgh throughout the late 1970s.

6. Dollard, *Caste and Class in a Southern Town,* 2d ed. (Garden City, N.Y., 1949), 93; Barry Goldberg, "Historical Reflections on Transnationalism, Race, and the American Immigrant Saga" (unpublished paper delivered at the Rethinking Migration, Race, Ethnicity, and Nationalism in Historical Perspective Conferences, New York Academy of the Sciences, May, 1990).

7. Albert S. Broussard, "George Albert Flippin and Race Relations in a Western Rural Community," *The Midwest Review,* 12 (1990): 15, n. 42; J. Alexander Karlin, "The Italo-American Incident of 1891 and the Road to Reunion," *Journal of Southern History,* 8 (1942); Gunther Peck, "Padrones and Protest: 'Old' Radicals and 'New' Immigrants in Bingham, Utah, 1905–1912," *Western Historical Quarterly,*

(May 1993): 177; Dan Georgakas, *Greek America at Work* (New York, 1992), 12 and 16–17; Yvette Huginnie, *Strikitos: Race, Class, and Work in the Arizona Copper Industry, 1870–1920*, Thesis (Ph.D.) Yale University, 1991.

   8. Donna Gabaccia, "The 'Yellow Peril' and the 'Chinese of Europe': Italian and Chinese Labourers in an International Labour Market" (unpublished paper, University of North Carolina at Charlotte, c. 1993).

   9. George E. Cunningham, "The Italian: A Hindrance to White Solidarity in Louisiana, 1890–1898," *Journal of Negro History*, 50 (January 1965): 34, includes the quotes.

   10. Higham, *Strangers in the Land*, 66; Gary R. Mormino and George E. Pozzetta, *The Immigrant World of Ybor City: Italians and Their Latin Neighbors in Tampa, 1885–1985* (Urbana, Ill., 1987), 241; Micaela DiLeonardo, *The Varieties of Ethnic Experience* (Ithaca, N.Y., 1984), 24, n. 16; Georgakas, *Greek America at Work*, 16. See also Karen Brodkin Sacks' superb "How Did Jews Become White Folks?" in Steven Gregory and Roger Sanjek, eds., *Race* (New Brunswick, N.J., 1994).

   11. Quoted in Brody, *Steelworkers*, 120; W. Lloyd Warner and J. O. Low, *The Social System of the Modern Factory. The Strike: A Social Analysis* (New Haven, 1947), 140; Gershon Legman, *The Horn Book* (New York, 1964), 486–87; *Anecdotal Americana: Five Hundred Stories for the Amusement of Five Hundred Nations That Comprise America* (New York, 1933), 98.

How Jews Became
White Folks

–Karen Brodkin

The American nation was founded and developed by the Nordic race, but if a few more million members of the Alpine, Mediterranean and Semitic races are poured among us, the result must inevitably be a hybrid race of people as worthless and futile as the good-for-nothing mongrels of Central America and Southeastern Europe.

Kenneth Roberts, in Carlson and Colburn 1972:312

It is clear that Kenneth Roberts did not think of my ancestors as white like him. The late nineteenth and early decades of the twentieth centuries saw a steady stream of warnings by scientists, policymakers, and the popular press that "mongrelization" of the Nordic or Anglo-Saxon race—the real Americans—by inferior European races (as well as inferior non-European ones) was destroying the fabric of the nation. I continue to be surprised to read that America did not always regard its immigrant European workers as white, that they thought people from different nations were biologically different. My parents, who are first-generation U.S.-born Eastern European Jews, are not surprised. They expect anti-Semitism to be part of the fabric of daily life, much as I expect racism to be part of it. They came of age in a Jewish world in the 1920s and 1930s at the peak of anti-Semitism in the United States (Gerber 1986). . . .

It is certainly true that the United States has a history of anti-Semitism and of beliefs that Jews were members of an inferior race. But Jews were hardly alone. American anti-Semitism was part of a broader pattern of late-nineteenth-century racism against all southern and eastern European immigrants, as well as against Asian immigrants. These views justified all sorts of discriminatory treatment including closing the doors to immigration from Europe and Asia in the 1920s.[1] This picture changed radically after World War II. Suddenly the same folks who promoted nativism and xenophobia were eager to believe that the Euro-origin people whom they had deported, reviled as members of inferior races, and prevented from immigrating only a few years earlier were now model middle-class white suburban citizens.

It was not an educational epiphany that made those in power change their hearts, their minds, and our race. Instead, it was the biggest and best affirmative action program in the history of our nation, and it was for Euromales. There are similarities and differences in the ways each of the European immigrant groups became "whitened." I want to tell the story in a way that links anti-Semitism to other varieties of anti-European racism, because this foregrounds what Jews shared with other Euroimmigrants and shows changing notions of whiteness to be part of America's larger system of institutional racism.

EURORACES

The U.S. "discovery" that Europe had inferior and superior races came in response to the great waves of immigration from southern and eastern Europe in the late nineteenth century. Before that time, European immigrants—including Jews—had been largely assimilated into the white population. The twenty-three million European immigrants who came to work in U.S. cities after 1880 were too many and too concentrated to disperse and blend. Instead, they piled up in the country's most dilapidated urban areas, where they built new kinds of working-class ethnic communities. Since immigrants and their children made up more than 70 percent of the population of most of the country's largest cities, urban America came to take on a distinctly immigrant flavor. The golden age of industrialization in the United States was also the golden age of class struggle between the captains of the new industrial empires and the masses of manual workers whose labor made them rich. As the majority of mining and manufacturing workers, immigrants were visibly major players in these struggles (Higham 1955:226; Steinberg 1989:36).[2]

The Red Scare of 1919 clearly linked anti-immigrant to anti-working-class sentiment—to the extent that the Seattle general strike of native-born workers was blamed on foreign agitators. The Red Scare was fueled by economic depression, a massive postwar strike wave, the Russian revolution, and a new wave of postwar immigration. Strikers in steel, and the garment and textile workers in New York and New England, were mainly new immigrants. "As part of a fierce counteroffensive, employers inflamed the historic identification of class conflict with immigrant radicalism." Anti-communism and anti-immigrant sentiment came together in the Palmer raids and deportation of immigrant working-class activists. There was real fear of revolution. One of President Wilson's aides feared it was "the first appearance of the soviet in this country" (Higham 1955:226).

Not surprisingly, the belief in European races took root most deeply among the wealthy U.S.-born Protestant elite, who feared a hostile and seemingly unassimilable working class. By the end of the nineteenth century, Senator Henry Cabot Lodge pressed Congress to cut off immigration to the United States; Teddy Roosevelt raised the alarm of "race suicide" and took Anglo-Saxon women to task for allowing "native" stock to be outbred by inferior immigrants. In the twentieth century, these fears gained a great deal of social legitimacy thanks to the efforts of an influential network of aristocrats and scientists who developed theories of eugenics—breeding for a "better" humanity—and scientific racism. Key to these efforts was Madison Grant's influential *Passing of the Great Race,* in which he shared his discovery that there were three or four major European races ranging from the superior Nordics of northwestern Europe to the inferior southern and eastern races of Alpines, Mediterraneans, and, worst of all, Jews, who seemed to be everywhere in his native New York City. Grant's nightmare was race mixing among Europeans. For him, "the cross between any of the three European races and a Jew is a Jew" (qtd. in Higham 1955:156). He didn't have good things to say about Alpine or Mediterranean "races" either. For Grant, race and class were interwoven: the upper class was racially pure Nordic, and the lower classes came from the lower races.

Far from being on the fringe, Grant's views resonated with those of the nonimmigrant middle class. A *New York Times* reporter wrote of his visit to the Lower East Side:

> This neighborhood, peopled almost entirely by the people who claim to have been driven from Poland and Russia, is the eyesore of New York and perhaps the filthiest place on the western continent. It is impossible for a Christian to live there because he will be driven out, either by blows or the dirt and stench. Cleanliness is an unknown quantity to these people. They cannot be lifted up to a higher plane because they do not want to be. If the cholera should ever get among these people, they would scatter its germs as a sower does grain. (qtd. in Schoener 1967:58)[3]

Such views were well within the mainstream of the early-twentieth-century scientific community. Grant and eugenicist Charles B. Davenport organized the Galton Society in 1918 in order to foster research and to otherwise promote eugenics and immigration restriction.[4] Lewis Terman, Henry Goddard, and Robert Yerkes, developers of the so-called intelligence test, believed firmly that southeastern European immigrants, African Americans, American Indians, and Mexicans were "feebleminded." And indeed, more than 80 percent of the immigrants whom Goddard tested at Ellis Island in 1912 turned out to be just that. Racism fused with eugenics in scientific circles, and the eugenics circles overlapped with the nativism of WASP aristocrats. During World War I, racism shaped the army's development of a mass intelligence test. Psychologist Robert Yerkes, who developed the test, became an even stronger advocate of eugenics after the war. Writing in the *Atlantic Monthly* in 1923, he noted:

> If we may safely judge by the army measurements of intelligence, races are quite as significantly different as individuals. . . . [and] almost as great as the intellectual difference between negro and white in the army are the differences between white racial groups. . . .
> For the past ten years or so the intellectual status of immigrants has been disquietingly low. Perhaps this is because of the dominance of the Mediterranean races, as contrasted with the Nordic and Alpine. (qtd. in Carlson and Colburn 1972:333–334)

By the 1920s, scientific racism sanctified the notion that real Americans were white and real whites came from northwest Europe. Racism animated laws excluding and expelling Chinese in 1882, and then closing the door to immigration by virtually all Asians and most Europeans in 1924 (Saxton 1971, 1990). Northwestern European ancestry as a requisite for whiteness was set in legal concrete when the Supreme Court denied Bhagat Singh Thind the right to become a naturalized citizen under a 1790 federal law that allowed whites the right to become naturalized citizens. Thind argued that Asian Indians were the real Aryans and Caucasians, and therefore white. The Court countered that the United States only wanted blond Aryans and Caucasians, "that the blond Scandinavian and the brown Hindu have a common ancestor in the dim reaches of antiquity, but the average man knows perfectly well that there are unmistakable and profound differences between them today" (Takaki 1989:298–299). A narrowly defined white, Christian race was also built into the 1705 Virginia "Act concerning servants and slaves." This statute stated "that no negroes, mulattos and Indians or other infidels or jews, Moors, Mahometans or other infidels shall, at any time, purchase any christian servant, nor any other except of their own complexion" (Martyn 1979:111).[5]

The 1930 census added its voice, distinguishing not only immigrant from "native" whites, but also native whites of native white parentage, and native whites of immigrant (or mixed) parentage. In distinguishing immigrant (southern and eastern Europeans) from "native" (northwestern Europeans), the census reflected the racial distinctions of the eugenicist-inspired intelligence tests.[6]

Racism and anti-immigrant sentiment in general and anti-Semitism in particular flourished in higher education. Jews were the first of the Euroimmigrant groups to enter colleges in significant numbers, so it wasn't surprising that they faced the brunt of discrimination there.[7] The Protestant elite complained that Jews were unwashed, uncouth, unrefined, loud, and pushy. Harvard University President A. Lawrence Lowell, who was also a vice president of the Immigration Restriction League, was openly opposed to Jews at Harvard. The Seven Sisters schools had a reputation for "flagrant discrimination." M. Carey Thomas, Bryn Mawr president, may have been a feminist of a kind, but she also was an admirer of scientific racism and an advocate of immigration restriction. She "blocked both the admission of black students and the promotion of Jewish instructors" (Synott 1986:233, 238–239, 249–250).

Anti-Semitic patterns set by these elite schools influenced standards of other schools, made anti-Semitism acceptable, and "made the aura of exclusivity a desirable commodity for the college-seeking clientele" (Synott 1986:250; and see Karabel 1984; Silberman 1985; Steinberg 1989: chaps. 5, 9). Fear that colleges "might soon be overrun by Jews" were publicly expressed at a 1918 meeting of the Association of New England Deans. In 1919 Columbia University took steps to decrease the number of entering Jews by a set of practices that soon came to be widely adopted. The school developed a psychological test based on the World War I army intelligence tests to measure "innate ability—and middle-class home environment" and redesigned the admission application to ask for religion, father's name and birthplace, a photo, and a personal interview (Synott 1986:239–240). Other techniques for excluding Jews, like a fixed class size, a chapel requirement, and preference for children of alumni were less obvious. Sociologist Jerome Karabel (1984) has argued that these exclusionary efforts provided the basis for contemporary criteria for college admission that mix grades and test scores with criteria for well-roundedness and character, as well as affirmative action for athletes and children of alumni, which allowed schools to select more affluent Protestants. Their proliferation in the 1920s caused the intended drop in the number of Jewish students in law, dental, and medical schools and also saw the imposition of quotas in engineering, pharmacy, and veterinary schools.[8]

* * *

EUROETHNICS INTO WHITES

By the time I was an adolescent, Jews were just as white as the next white person. Until I was eight, I was a Jew in a world of Jews. Everyone on Avenue Z in Sheepshead Bay was Jewish. I spent my days playing and going to school on three blocks of Avenue Z, and visiting my grandparents in the nearby Jewish neighborhoods of Brighton Beach and Coney Island. There were plenty of Italians in my neighborhood, but they lived around the corner. They were a kind of Jew, but on the margins of my social horizons. Portugese were even more distant, at the end of the bus ride, at Sheepshead Bay. The schul, or temple, was on Avenue Z, and I begged my father to take me like all the other fathers took their kids, but religion wasn't part of my family's Judaism. Just how Jewish my neighborhood was hit me in first grade when I was one of two kids in my class to go to school on Rosh Hashanah. My teacher was shocked—she was Jewish too—and I was embarrassed to tears when she sent me home. I was never again sent to school on Jewish holidays. We left that world in 1949 when we moved to Valley Stream, Long Island, which was Protestant, Republican, and even had farms until Irish, Italian, and Jewish exurbanites like us gave it a more suburban and Democratic flavor. Neither religion nor ethnicity separated us at school or in the neighborhood. Except temporarily. In elementary school years, I remember a fair number of dirt-bomb (a good suburban weapon) wars on the block. Periodically one of the Catholic boys would accuse me or my brother of killing his God, to which we would reply, "Did not" and start lobbing dirt-bombs. Sometimes he would get his friends from Catholic school, and I would get mine from public school kids on the block, some of whom were Catholic. Hostilities lasted no more than a couple of hours and punctuated an otherwise friendly relationship. They ended by junior high years, when other things became more important. Jews, Catholics, and Protestants, Italians, Irish, Poles, and "English" (I don't remember hearing WASP as a kid) were mixed up on the block and in school. We thought of ourselves as middle class and very enlightened because our ethnic backgrounds seemed so irrelevant to high school culture. We didn't see race (we thought), and racism was not part of our peer consciousness, nor were the immigrant or working-class histories of our families.

Like most chicken and egg problems, it's hard to know which came first. Did Jews and other Euroethnics become white because they became middle class? That is, did money whiten? Or did being incorporated in an expanded version of whiteness open up the economic doors to a middle-class status? Clearly, both tendencies were at work. Some of the changes set in motion during the war against fascism led to a more inclusive version of whiteness. Anti-Semitism and anti-European racism lost respectability. The 1940 census no longer distinguished native whites of native parentage from those, like my parents, of immigrant parentage, so that Euroimmigrants and their children were more securely white by submersion in an expanded notion of whiteness. (This census also changed the race of Mexicans to white [U.S. Bureau of the Census, 1940:4].) Theories of nurture and culture replaced theories of nature and biology. Instead of dirty and dangerous races who would destroy U.S. democracy, immigrants became ethnic groups whose children had successfully assimilated into the mainstream and risen to the middle class. In this new myth, Euroethnic suburbs like mine became the measure of U.S. democracy's victory over racism. Jewish mobility became a new Horatio Alger story. In time and with hard work, every ethnic group would get a piece of the pie, and the United States would be a nation with equal opportunity for all its people to become part of a prosperous middle-class majority. And it seemed that Euroethnic immigrants and their children were delighted to join middle America[9]. . . .

Although changing views on who was white made it easier for Euroethnics to become middle class, it was also the case that economic prosperity played a very powerful role in the whitening process. Economic mobility of Jews and other Euroethnics rested ultimately on U.S. postwar economic prosperity with its enormously expanded need for professional, technical, and managerial labor, and on government assistance in providing it. The United States emerged from the war with the strongest economy in the world. Real wages rose between 1946 and 1960, increasing buying power a hefty 22 percent and giving most Americans some discretionary income (Nash et al. 1986:885–886). U.S. manufacturing, banking, and business services became increasingly dominated by large corporations, and these grew into multinational corporations. Their organizational centers lay in big, new urban headquarters that demanded growing numbers of technical and managerial workers. The postwar period was a historic moment for real class mobility and for the affluence we have erroneously come to believe was the U.S. norm. It was a time when the old white and the newly white masses became middle class.

The GI Bill of Rights, as the 1944 Serviceman's Readjustment Act was known, was arguably the most massive affirmative action program in U.S. history. It was created to develop needed labor-force skills, and to provide those who had them with a life-style that reflected their value to the economy. The GI benefits ultimately extended to sixteen million GIs (veterans of the Korean War as well) included priority in jobs—that is, preferential hiring, but no one objected to it then—financial support during the job search; small loans for starting up businesses; and, most important, low-interest home loans and educational benefits, which included tuition and living expenses (Brown 1946; Hurd 1946; Mosch 1975; *Postwar Jobs for Veterans* 1945; Willenz 1983). This legislation was rightly regarded as one of the most revolutionary postwar programs. I call it affirmative action because it was aimed at and disproportionately helped male, Euro-origin GIs.

GI benefits, like the New Deal affirmative action programs before them and the 1960s affirmative action programs after them, were responses to protest. Business executives and the general public believed that the war economy had only temporarily halted the Great Depression. Many feared its return and a return to the labor strife and radicalism of the 1930s (Eichler 1982:4; Nash et al. 1986:885). "[M]emories of the Depression remained vivid and many people suffered from what Davis Ross has aptly called 'depression psychosis'—the fear that the war would inevitably be followed by layoffs and mass unemployment" (Wynn 1976:15).

It was a reasonable fear. The eleven million military personnel who were demobilized in the 1940s represented a quarter of the U.S. labor force (Mosch 1975:1, 20). In addition, ending war production brought a huge number of layoffs, growing unemployment, and a high rate of inflation. To recoup wartime losses in real wages caused by inflation as well as by the unions' no-strike pledge in support of the war effort, workers staged a massive wave of strikes in 1946. More workers went out on strike that year than ever before, and there were strikes in all the heavy industries: railroads, coal mining, auto, steel, and electrical. For a brief moment, it looked like class struggle all over again. But government and business leaders had learned from the experience of bitter labor struggles after World War I just how important it was to assist demobilized soldiers. The GI Bill resulted from their determination to avoid those mistakes this time. The biggest benefits of this legislation were for college and technical school education, and for very cheap home mortgages.

EDUCATION AND OCCUPATION

It is important to remember that prior to the war, a college degree was still very much a "mark of the upper class" (Willenz 1983:165). Colleges were largely finishing schools for Protestant elites. Before the postwar boom, schools could not begin to accommodate the American masses. Even in New York City before the 1930s, neither the public schools nor City College had room for more than a tiny fraction of potential immigrant students.

Not so after the war. The almost eight million GIs who took advantage of their educational benefits under the GI bill caused "the greatest wave of college building in American history" (Nash et al. 1986:885). White male GIs were able to take advantage of their educational benefits for college and technical training, so they were particularly well positioned to seize the opportunities provided by the new demands for professional, managerial, and technical labor. "It has been well documented that the GI educational benefits transformed American higher education and raised the educational level of that generation and generations to come. With many provisions for assistance in upgrading their educational attainments veterans pulled ahead of nonveterans in earning capacity. In the long run it was the nonveterans who had fewer opportunities" (Willenz 1983:165).[10]

Just how valuable a college education was for white men's occupational mobility can be seen in John Keller's study of who benefited from the metamorphosis of California's Santa Clara Valley into Silicon Valley. Formerly an agricultural region, in the 1950s the area became the scene of explosive growth in the semiconductor electronics industry. This industry epitomized the postwar economy and occupational structure. It owed its existence directly to the military and to the National Aeronautics and Space Administration (NASA), who were its major funders and its major markets. It had an increasingly white-collar work force. White men, who were the initial production workers in the 1950s, quickly transformed themselves into a technical and professional work force thanks largely to GI benefits and the new junior college training programs designed to meet the industry's growing work-force needs. Keller notes that "62 percent of enrollees at San Jose Junior College (later renamed San Jose City College) came from blue-collar families, and 55 percent of all job placements were as electronics technicians in the industrial and service sectors of the country economy" (1983:363). As white men left assembly work and the industry expanded between 1950 and 1960, they were replaced initially by Latinas and African-American women, who were joined after 1970 by new immigrant women. Inmigrating men tended to work in the better-paid unionized industries that grew up in the area (Keller 1983:346–373). . . .

Educational and occupational GI benefits really constituted affirmative action programs for white males because they were decidedly not extended to African Americans or to women of any race. White male privilege was shaped against the backdrop of wartime racism and postwar sexism. During and after the war, there was an upsurge in white racist violence against black servicemen in public schools, and in the KKK, which spread to California and New York (Dalfiume 1969:133–134). The number of lynchings rose during the war, and in 1943 there were antiblack race riots in several large northern cities. Although there was a wartime labor shortage, black people were discriminated against in access to well-paid defense industry jobs and in housing. In 1946 there were white riots against African Americans across the South, and in Chicago and Philadelphia as well. Gains made as a result of the wartime Civil Rights movement, especially employment in defense-related industries, were lost with peacetime conversion as black workers were the first fired, often in violation of seniority (Wynn 1976:114, 116). White women were also laid off, ostensibly to make jobs for demobilized servicemen, and in the long run women lost most of the gains they had made in wartime (Kessler-Harris 1982). We now know that women did not leave the labor force in any significant numbers but instead were forced to find inferior jobs, largely nonunion, part-time, and clerical.

Theoretically available to all veterans, in practice women and black veterans did not get anywhere near their share of GI benefits. Because women's units were not treated as part of the military, women in them were not considered veterans and were ineligible for Veterans' Administration (VA) benefits (Willenz 1983:168). The barriers that almost completely shut African-American GIs out of their benefits were more complex. In Wynn's portrait (1976:115), black GIs anticipated starting new lives, just like their white counterparts. Over 43 percent hoped to return to school and most expected to relocate to find better jobs in new lines of work. The exodus from the South toward the North and far West was particularly large. So it wasn't a question of any lack of ambition on the part of African-American GIs.

Rather, the military, the Veterans' Administration, the U.S. Employment Service, and the Federal Housing Administration (FHA) effectively denied African-American GIs access to their benefits and to the new educational, occupational, and residential opportunities. Black GIs who served in the thoroughly segregated armed forces during World War II served under white officers, usually southerners (Binkin and Eitelberg 1982; Dalfiume 1969; Foner 1974; Johnson 1967; Nalty and MacGregor

1981). African-American soldiers were disproportionately given dishonorable discharges, which denied them veterans' rights under the GI Bill. Thus between August and November 1946, 21 percent of white soldiers and 39 percent of black soldiers were dishonorably discharged. Those who did get an honorable discharge then faced the Veterans' Administration and the U.S. Employment Service. The latter, which was responsible for job placements, employed very few African Americans, especially in the South. This meant that black veterans did not receive much employment information, and that the offers they did receive were for low-paid and menial jobs. "In one survey of 50 cities, the movement of blacks into peacetime employment was found to be lagging far behind that of white veterans: in Arkansas 95 percent of the placements made by the USES for Afro-Americans were in service or unskilled jobs" (Nalty and MacGregor 1981:218, and see 60–61). African Americans were also less likely than whites, regardless of GI status, to gain new jobs commensurate with their wartime jobs, and they suffered more heavily. For example, in San Francisco by 1948, Black Americans "had dropped back halfway to their prewar employment status" (Wynn 1976:114, 116).[11]

Black GIs faced discrimination in the educational system as well. Despite the end of restrictions on Jews and other Euroethnics, African Americans were not welcome in white colleges. Black colleges were overcrowded, and the combination of segregation and prejudice made for few alternatives. About twenty thousand black veterans attended college by 1947, most in black colleges, but almost as many, fifteen thousand could not gain entry. Predictably, the disproportionately few African Americans who did gain access to their educational benefits were able, like their white counterparts, to become doctors and engineers, and to enter the black middle class (Walker 1970).

*   *   *

The record is very clear that instead of seizing the opportunity to end institutionalized racism, the federal government did its best to shut and double seal the postwar window of opportunity in African Americans' faces. It consistently refused to combat segregation in the social institutions that were key for upward mobility: education, housing, and employment. Moreover, federal programs that were themselves designed to assist demobilized GIs and young families systematically discriminated against African Americans. Such programs reinforced white/nonwhite racial distinctions even as intrawhite racialization was falling out of fashion. This other side of the coin, that white men of northwestern and southeastern European ancestry were treated equally in theory and in practice with regard to the benefits they received, was part of the larger postwar whitening of Jews and other eastern and southern Europeans.

The myth that Jews pulled themselves up by their own bootstraps ignores the fact that it took federal programs to create the conditions whereby the abilities of Jews and other European immigrants could be recognized and rewarded rather than denigrated and denied. The GI Bill and FHA and VA mortgages were forms of affirmative action that allowed male Jews and other Euro-American men to become suburban homeowners and to get the training that allowed them—but not women vets or war workers—to become professionals, technicians, salesmen, and managers in a growing economy. Jews' and other white ethnics' upward mobility was the result of programs that allowed us to float on a rising economic tide. To African Americans, the government offered the cement boots of segregation, redlining, urban renewal, and discrimination.

Those racially skewed gains have been passed across the generations, so that racial inequality seems to maintain itself "naturally," even after legal segregation ended. Today, in a shrinking economy where downward mobility is the norm, the children and grandchildren of the postwar beneficiaries of the economic boom have some precious advantages. For example, having parents who own their own homes or who have decent retirement benefits can make a real difference in young people's ability to take on huge college loans or to come up with a down payment for a house. Even this simple inheritance helps perpetuate the gap between whites and nonwhites. Sure Jews needed ability, but ability was not enough to make it. The same applies even more in today's long recession.

NOTES

This is a revised and expanded version of a paper published in *Jewish Currents* in June 1992 and delivered at the 1992 meetings of the American Anthropological Association in the session *Blacks and Jews, 1992: Reaching across the Cultural Boundaries* organized by Angela Gilliam. I would like to thank Emily Abel, Katya Gibel Azoulay, Edna Bonacich, Angela Gilliam, Isabelle Gunning, Valerie Matsumoto, Regina Morantz-Sanchez, Roger Sanjek, Rabbi Chaim Scidler-Feller, Janet Silverstein, and Eloise Klein Hoaly's writing group for uncovering wonderful sources and for critical readings along the way.

1. Indeed, Boasian and Du Boisian anthropology developed in active political opposition to this nativism; on Du Bois, see Harrison and Nonini 1992.

2. On immigrants as part of the industrial work force, see Steinberg 1989:36.

3. I thank Roger Sanjek for providing me with this source.

4. It was intended, as Davenport wrote to the president of the American Museum of Natural History, Henry Fairfield Osborne, as "an anthropological society . . . with a central governing body, self-elected and self-perpetuating, and very limited in members, and also confined to native Americans who are anthropologically, socially and politically sound, no Bolsheviki need apply" (Barkan 1991:67–68).

5. I thank Valerie Matsumoto for telling me about the Thind case and Katya Gibel Azoulay for providing this information to me on the Virginia statute.

6. "The distinction between white and colored" has been "the only racial classification which has been carried through all the 15 censuses." "Colored" consisted

of "Negroes" and "other races": Mexican, Indian, Chinese, Japanese, Filipino, Hindu, Korean, Hawaiian, Malay, Siamese, and Samoan (U.S. Bureau of the Census, 1930:25, 26).

7. For why Jews entered colleges earlier than other immigrants, and for a challenge to views that attribute it to Jewish culture, see Steinberg 1989.

8. Although quotas on Jews persisted into the 1950s in some of the elite schools, they were much attenuated, as the postwar college-building boom gave the coup-de-grace to the gentleman's finishing school.

9. Indeed, Jewish social scientists were prominent in creating this ideology of the United States as a meritocracy. Most prominent of course was Nathan Glazer, but among them also were Charles Silberman and Marshall Sklare.

10. The belief was widespread that "the GI Bill . . . helped millions of families move into the middle class" (Nash et al. 1986:885). A study that compares mobility among veterans and nonveterans provides a kind of confirmation. In an unnamed small city in Illinois, Havighurst and his colleagues (1951) found no significant difference between veterans and nonveterans, but this was because apparently very few veterans used any of their GI benefits.

11. African Americans and Japanese Americans were the main target of wartime racism (see Murray 1992). By contrast, there were virtually no anti-German American or anti-Italian American policies in World War II (see Takaki 1989:357–406).

REFERENCES

Barkan, Elazar. 1991. *The Retreat of Scientific Racism: Changing Concepts of Race in Britain and the United States between the World Wars*. Cambridge: Cambridge University Press.

Binkin, Martin, and Mark J. Eitelberg. 1982. *Blacks and the Military*. Washington, D.C.: Brookings.

Brown, Francis J. 1946. *Educational Opportunities for Veterans*. Washington, D.C.: Public Affairs Press, American Council on Public Affairs.

Carlson, Lewis H., and George A. Colburn. 1972. *In Their Place: White America Defines Her Minorities, 1850–1950*. New York: Wiley.

Dalfiume, Richard M. 1969. *Desegregation of the U.S. Armed Forces: Fighting on Two Fronts, 1939–1953*. Columbia: University of Missouri Press.

Eichler, Ned. 1982. *The Merchant Builders*. Cambridge, Mass.: MIT Press.

Foner, Jack. 1974. *Blacks and the Military in American History: A New Perspective*. New York: Praeger.

Gerber, David. 1986. Introduction. In *Anti-Semitism in American History*, ed. Gerber. Urbana: University of Illinois Press, 3–56.

Harrison, Faye V., and Donald Nonini, eds. 1992. *Critique of Anthropology* (special issue on W.E.B. Du Bois and anthropology) 12(3).

Havighurst, Robert J., John W. Baughman, Walter H. Eaton, and Ernest W. Burgess. 1951. *The American Veteran Back Home: A Study of Veteran Readjustment*. New York: Longmans, Green.

Higham, John. 1955. *Strangers in the Land*. New Brunswick: Rutgers University Press.

Hurd, Charles. 1946. *The Veterans' Program: A Complete Guide to Its Benefits, Rights, and Options.* New York: McGraw-Hill.

Johnson, Jesse J. 1967. *Ebony Brass: An Autobiography of Negro Frustration amid Aspiration.* New York: Frederick.

Karabel, Jerome. 1984. Status-Group Struggle, Organizational Interests, and the Limits of Institutional Autonomy. *Theory and Society* 13:1–40.

Keller, John F. 1983. The Division of Labor in Electronics. In *Women, Men, and the International Division of Labor,* ed. June Nash and Maria Patricia Fernandez-Kelly. Albany: SUNY Press, 346–373.

Kessler-Harris, Alice. 1982. *Out to Work: A History of Wage-Earning Women in the United States.* New York: Oxford University Press.

Martyn, Byron Curti. 1979. Racism in the U.S.: A History of Anti-Miscegenation Legislation and Litigation. Ph.D. diss., University of Southern California.

Mosch, Theodore R. 1975. *The GI Bill: A Breakthrough in Educational and Social Policy in the United States.* Hicksville, N.Y.: Exposition.

Murray, Alice Yang. 1992. Japanese Americans, Redress, and Reparations: A Study of Community, Family, and Gender, 1940–1990. Ph. D. diss., Stanford University.

Nalty, Bernard C., and Morris J. MacGregor, eds. 1981. *Blacks in the Military: Essential Documents.* Wilmington, Del.: Scholarly Resources.

Nash, Gary B., Julie Roy Jeffrey, John R. Howe, Allen F. Davis, Peter J. Frederick, and Allen M. Winkler. 1986. *The American People: Creating a Nation and a Society.* New York: Harper and Row.

Postwar Jobs for Veterans. 1945. *Annals of the American Academy of Political and Social Science* 238 (March).

Saxton, Alexander. 1971. *The Indispensible Enemy.* Berkeley and Los Angeles: University of California Press.

Schoener, Allon. 1967. *Portal to America: The Lower East Side, 1870–1925.* New York: Holt, Rinehart and Winston.

Sifry, Micah. 1993. Anti-Semitism in America. *Nation,* January 25, 92–99.

Silberman, Charles. 1985. *A Certain People: American Jews and Their Lives Today.* New York: Summit.

Sklare, Marshall. 1971. *America's Jews.* New York: Random House.

Steinberg, Stephen. 1989. *The Ethnic Myth: Race, Ethnicity, and Class in America.* 2d ed. Boston: Beacon.

Synott, Marcia Graham. 1986. Anti-Semitism and American Universities: Did Quotas Follow the Jews? In *Anti-Semitism in American History,* ed. David A. Gerber. Urbana: University of Illinois Press, 233–274.

Takaki, Ronald. 1989. *Strangers from a Different Shore.* Boston: Little, Brown.

U.S. Bureau of the Census. 1930. *Fifteenth Census of the United States.* Vol. 2. Washington D.C.: U.S. Government Printing Office.

———. 1940. *Sixteenth Census of the United States.* Vol. 2. Washington D.C.: U.S. Government Printing Office.

Walker, Olive. 1970. The Windsor Hills School Story. *Integrated Education: Race and Schools* 8(3):4–9.

Willenz, June A. 1983. *Women Veterans: America's Forgotten Heroines.* New York: Continuum.

Wynn, Neil A. 1976. *The Afro-American and the Second World War.* London: Elek.

chapterfive

Becoming Hispanic: Mexican Americans and Whiteness

–Neil Foley

In 1980 the U.S. Bureau of the Census created two new ethnic categories of Whites: "Hispanic" and "non-Hispanic." The Hispanic category, an ethnic rather than racial label, comprised Mexicans, Puerto Ricans, Cubans, Panamanians, and other ethnic groups of Latin American descent. Creating a separate ethnic category within the racial category of White seemed to solve the problem of how to count Hispanics without racializing them as non-Whites, as it had done in 1930. To identify oneself today as a "Hispanic" is partially to acknowledge one's ethnic heritage without surrendering one's "whiteness." Hispanic identity thus implies a kind of "separate but equal" whiteness—whiteness with a twist of salsa, enough to make one ethnically flavorful and culturally exotic without, however, compromising one's racial privilege as a White person. The history of Mexican Americans in the Southwest is thus more than the history of their "becoming" Mexican American or Hispanic; for many, especially those of the middle class, it is also the history of their becoming White.

Unlike Black Americans, who experienced de jure segregation throughout the South before 1960, Mexican Americans in the Southwest experienced de facto segregation based on custom rather than statutory authority. Legally, Mexican Americans were accorded the racial status of White people; socially, politically, and economically, however, they were treated as non-Whites. With the rise of the so-called Mexican American generation of the 1930s, '40s, and '50s, Mexican Americans began insisting on their status as Whites in order to overcome the worst features of Jim Crow segregation, restrictive housing covenants, employment

59

discrimination, and the social stigma of being "Mexican," a label that, in the eyes of Anglos, designated race rather than one's citizenship status.

Many middle-class Mexican Americans did not object to the segregation of Blacks or challenge the assumptions of White supremacy. On the contrary, they supported strict segregation of Whites and Blacks in the schools and in public facilities. The basis for their claim for social equality was that they were also White, that some unfortunate mistake had been made in regarding persons of Mexican descent as non-Whites.

A group of Mexican Americans, mostly urban and middle class, founded their own organization in 1929 in Corpus Christi, the League of United Latin American Citizens (LULAC), to foster the goals of Americanization in Texas and other states of the Southwest, restricting membership to U.S. citizens and emphasizing English language skills and loyalty to the Constitution of the United States. LULAC members sought to set the racial record straight. In a 1932 article in the *LULAC News* titled "Are Texas-Mexicans 'Americans'?" the author asserted that Mexican Americans were "the first white race to inhabit this vast empire of ours." Another member of LULAC boasted that Mexican Americans were "not only a part and parcel but as well the sum and substance of the white race." As self-constituted Whites, LULAC members considered it "an insult" to be associated with Blacks or other "colored" races.[1] In 1936 a LULAC official deplored the practice of hiring "Negro musicians" to play at Mexican *bailes* (dances) because it led to "illicit relations" between Black men and "ill-informed Mexican girls." He urged fellow LULAC members to "tell these Negroes that we are not going to permit our manhood and womanhood to mingle with them on an equal social basis."[2] Not surprisingly, therefore, LULAC, the premiere civil rights group for Mexican Americans, turned its back on opportunities to forge ties with the NAACP during its own civil rights battles in the 1940s and 1950s. The African American author and Nobel Prize winner Toni Morrison deserves credit for stating bluntly what many Mexican Americans have been slow to acknowledge: "In race talk the move into mainstream America always means buying into the notion of American blacks as the real aliens."[3]

Of course, African Americans are not "aliens" in any legal or cultural sense; they are natives of the United States, share in intimate ways the culture and history of the United States, and in many important respects have shaped White culture. W. E. B. Du Bois wrote that he saw through the "souls of white folks": "Not as a foreigner do I come, for I am native, not foreign. . . . I see the working of their entrails. I know their thoughts and they know that I know."[4] Blacks are inside American culture, but Morrison's point is that they remain alienated and estranged from the domain of White power and privilege. Mexican immigrants may begin as racial outsiders and "illegal aliens," but their U.S.-born offspring are sometimes able to forge identities as ethnically White Hispanics.

Unlike the experience of most immigrants, however, discrimination against Mexicans in the United States has been continuous, pervasive, and systemic. After Mexican Americans established LULAC and the G.I. Forum (founded in 1948), they challenged school segregation and other forms of discrimination in state and federal courts. While these organizations and their middle-class Mexican American leaders sought equality based on their constitutional rights as U.S. citizens, increasingly they came to the realization that race—specifically, being White—mattered far more than U.S. citizenship in the course of everyday life. The majority of people of African descent in the United States were citizens, but that fact did not enable them to sit in the front of the bus or attend White schools. As sociologist Mary Waters observed, "If the Irish had to sit at the back of the bus sometime in the past, and now being Irish just means having fun at funerals, then there is hope for all groups facing discrimination now."[5] The assumption here is that most immigrant groups, including Mexicans, have had the "option," unlike Blacks, of becoming White and thus benefiting from what historian George Lipsitz has called the "possessive investment in whiteness."[6] Choosing the Caucasian option, as had the Irish before them, enabled some Mexican Americans to forge White racial identities that were constructed, as Toni Morrison has accurately observed, "on the backs of blacks."[7]

Having failed to convince Anglos that the word "Mexican" denoted nationality rather than a separate race, LULAC members and other urban Mexican Americans constructed new identities as "Spanish American" or "Latin American" in order to arrogate to themselves the privileges of whiteness routinely denied to Mexicans, Blacks, Chinese, and Indians. Becoming Spanish or Latin American also enabled Mexican Americans to distance themselves from recently arrived Mexican immigrants who were often illiterate, poor, non-English speaking, and dark skinned. Mexican Americans thus began to object strenuously to being labeled as "colored" or forced to share facilities with Black Americans. Increasingly, middle-class Mexican Americans during the thirties and forties began to call themselves "Spanish" and insist on their whiteness. . . .

Many Mexicans had learned whiteness and "whitening" (*blanqueamiento*) before coming to the United States. Long-term interaction among African, indigenous, and Spanish peoples had led to the formation of a complex, hierarchical racial system in Mexico. After centuries of *mestizaje*, or race-mixing, society in colonial New Spain was composed of multiple ethnoracial groups. By the early twentieth century, the Mexican government had created census categories for three racial groups: Whites, Indians, and mestizos. The population of Mexico in 1920 consisted of about 14 million: 10 percent were classified as *raza blanca* (Whites), 30 percent as *raza indígena* (Indians), and about 60 percent as *raza mezclada* (mestizos).[8] Mestizos had occupied an awkward position in this racial hierarchy, often hated by the Spanish for being part Indian and shunned by the Indians for being part

Spanish. Those able to construct identities as Spaniards often regarded mestizos, Indians, and Africans with racial contempt. By the end of the nineteenth century, however, many urban mestizo elites claimed to be Spanish, or mostly Spanish, in order to establish racial and cultural distance between themselves and Indians. . . .

Some Mexican Americans were therefore mortified when Anglo Americans made no effort to distinguish between "Spanish" or "White" Mexicans and "Indian" Mexicans, which also became a source of irritation to the Mexican government. Mexican consuls frequently complained that Mexican citizens were not being treated like White people in the United States. In 1933 the Mexican consul in Dallas wrote a county sheriff to protest that a Mexican citizen had been jailed "with the negro prisoners" instead of with the Anglos. "It is my opinion," the Mexican consul general wrote to the sheriff, "that there is no reason for segregating Mexicans from white Americans, inasmuch as they are both of the white race."[9]

The different views of the Texas sheriff and the Mexican consul over the racial status of Mexicans in the United States reflected their countries' legal and cultural perspectives on the issue of race mixing. For Mexicans, theoretically at least, *mestizaje* produced racial strength. The fusion of Spanish, Indian, and African created a race of people that was greater than the sum of its parts, what the Mexican philosopher José Vasconcelos called the "cosmic race." To the Texas sheriff and the average White person in America, however, race mixing was a menace to the purity of the Nordic race that, unchecked, would lead to the demise of White civilization. When Spaniards mixed their blood with Indians and Africans, White Americans believed, they removed themselves from the domain of whiteness. This "dark stream" of "peon blood" was inferior to even that of southern European Jews and Slavs whom the eugenicist Madison Grant accused of producing "race bastards" and other "amazing racial hybrids" and "ethnic horrors that will be beyond the powers of future anthropologists to unravel."[10]

The history of discrimination against Mexican Americans in the Southwest is a thrice-told tale and does not bear repetition here. What is key, however, is the way in which the courts and the census constructed whiteness and the often conflicting and contradictory way in which Whites themselves constructed it. Historically, if not legally, Mexicans had been regarded as non-White and denied most of the rights and privileges that whiteness bestowed. In school segregation cases, however, the courts uniformly ruled that Mexicans belonged to the White race; and in the one naturalization case concerning a Mexican American, the court ruled that Mexican citizens, regardless of race, were entitled to become U.S. citizens as a result of treaty agreements. Mexican Americans reasoned that if the law said they were White, then Anglos broke the law by discriminating against them as non-Whites. . . .

The Supreme Court acknowledged that many immigrants from eastern and southern Europe who were considered White in the 1920s—Italians, Greeks, Slavs, and Jews, for example—were outside the bounds of whiteness in 1790 and had only later been granted status as Whites. The courts, especially those adjudicating whiteness for the purpose of naturalization, often relied on "common knowledge," or how the average White person viewed the whiteness of a person. Between 1878 and 1909 the courts heard twelve prerequisite or naturalization cases to determine whether a person seeking U.S. citizenship was White or not. In eleven of the cases, the courts barred the naturalization of applicants from China, Japan, Burma, and Hawaii, as well as that of two mixed-race applicants. As in other prerequisite cases, the applicants sought to convince the court that they met the racial criteria of whiteness by either scientific evidence (the division of humans into five racial groups: Mongolian, Negro, Caucasian, Indian, and Malay) or "common knowledge." The courts used either or both of these criteria to decide who was White and who was not. Takao Ozawa, a Japanese citizen educated at the University of California at Berkeley and resident of the United States for twenty-eight years, petitioned the court to become a citizen on the grounds that his skin color made him a "white person." The court disagreed with this literal interpretation of whiteness and in 1923 denied him citizenship on the grounds that he was of the Mongolian, not the Caucasian, race. White skin, by itself, did not guarantee one's "property right" in whiteness.[11]

Three months after ruling that Japanese were not Caucasian and therefore not White, the Supreme Court in *United States v. Thind* (1923) rejected its own equation that only Caucasians were White. Bhagat Singh Thind, one of approximately 6,400 Asian Indians in the United States by 1920, applied for citizenship on the grounds that Asian Indians were Caucasian and not Mongolian, were therefore White, and were therefore eligible for citizenship. The court did not dispute that Thind was a Caucasian but ruled that not all Caucasians were White despite the technical link between Europeans and South Asians. "It may be true," the court ruled, "that the blond Scandinavian and the brown Hindu have a common ancestor in the dim reaches of antiquity, but the average man knows perfectly well that there are unmistakable and profound differences between them today."[12] The Supreme Court thus ruled in the same year that Takao Ozawa was not White because, although he had white skin, he was not of the Caucasian race, whereas Bhagat Singh Thind was denied citizenship on the grounds that, although he was a Caucasian, he was not White. Whiteness, the courts increasingly ruled, was whatever they said it was. The Third ruling was the Supreme Court's final concession to the subjective, cultural construction of whiteness. . . .

To many Whites it must have seemed long overdue when the census bureau announced in 1930 that it had created a separate category for Mexicans. For the first time in census history, Mexicans had become racialized as a non-White group. The absence of a separate classification for persons of Mexican descent before 1930 had prevented immigration restrictionists and antirestrictionists alike from knowing the demographic dimensions of the "Mexican problem" during the 1920s when immigration restriction was hotly debated in Congress.[13] Accordingly, the instructions to the enumerators for the 1930 census stated: "Practically all Mexican laborers are of a racial mixture difficult to classify, though usually well recognized in the localities where they are found. In order to obtain separate figures for this racial group, it has been decided that all persons born in Mexico, or having parents born in Mexico, *who are not definitely white,* negro, Indian, Chinese, or Japanese, should be returned as Mexican.[14] Unlike census instructions before and after 1930, the 1930 census presumed Mexicans to be non-White unless "definitely white." Although no instructions were given to determine who was and who was not "definitely white," enumerators had to decide which Mexicans to count as Whites and which to enter in the non-White "Mexican" column. The outcome, not surprisingly, was that over 1.4 million persons were returned as "Mexicans" and therefore non-White, while only 65,986 (4 percent) of persons of Mexican descent were listed as White.[15] The majority of Mexicans in the United States were therefore recognized by the census, if not the courts, as non-Whites. Both the Mexican government and many Mexican Americans objected strenuously to the new classification scheme, and much to the dismay of eugenicists and assorted nativists, the census abandoned the category in subsequent censuses. Although having their whiteness restored did not lessen discrimination, the Mexican government and Mexican Americans fully understood the implications of being officially or legally recognized as a non-White group.

Segregation statutes consistently defined all those without African ancestry as "whites." Texas, for example, defined "colored children" as persons of mixed blood descended from "negro ancestry" for purposes of its school segregation laws and defined all persons besides those of African descent as White for purposes of its antimiscegenation and Jim Crow laws.[16] Chinese and Mexicans in Texas were thus White under state laws governing the segregation of the races, although in practice Mexicans were segregated into "Mexican schools" on the grounds that they needed special language instruction, were "dirty," or had fallen too far behind to be educated with Anglos of the same age.

In Texas the line between de jure and de facto segregation became increasingly blurred as school officials made decisions about district boundaries, school construction, transportation, and so forth that resulted in segregation of Mexican children from White schools. In the absence of statutory segregation that existed in the South between whites and blacks, Mexican Americans first challenged school segregation in 1930, the same year in which they achieved segregated status in the census. In *Independent School District v. Salvatierra* (1930), the Mexican American plaintiffs of Del

Rio, Texas, sought to prove that the actions taken by school officials were designed to accomplish "the complete segregation of the school children of Mexican and Spanish descent . . . from the school children of *all other white races* in the same grade." This clever wording recognized that Mexicans were not White in the sense that Anglos were, but that they belonged to a parallel universe of whiteness. The Texas Court of Civil Appeals agreed with the plaintiffs and ruled that "school authorities have no power to arbitrarily segregate Mexican children, assign them to separate schools, and exclude them from schools maintained for children of *other white races,* merely or solely because they are Mexicans."[17] However, it was a Pyrrhic victory for Mexicans because the court also affirmed the principle that children could be segregated if they had language difficulties or if as migrant workers they started school late. School officials were barred only from segregating Mexican children arbitrarily.

Mexican Americans had learned that the courts ended officially sanctioned segregation of Mexicans only when they insisted on their status as Whites. But how was one to become de facto White as well as de jure White? LULAC members had tried just about everything they could to prove how Americanized they were: they spoke English, voted, used the court systems, got elected to office, actively opposed Mexican immigration, and excluded Mexican citizens from membership in LULAC. They organized baseball teams and ate quantities of hot dogs. What more could they do to assimilate whiteness? Assimilation, however, is not only about what one leaves behind; it is also about what one is moving toward, what one acquires in the process of cultural exchange and fusion.

For many immigrant groups, assimilation, in part, meant becoming "American," which is also to say, becoming White. And becoming White, Toni Morrison has written, means that "A hostile posture toward resident blacks must be struck at the Americanizing door before it will open," adding that African Americans have historically served the "less than covert function of defining whites as the 'true' Americans."[18] As with other ethnic groups in the past—Italians, Poles, and Irish, for example—for Mexican Americans the path to whiteness involved not so much losing one's culture as becoming wedded to the notion that people of African descent were culturally and biologically inferior to Whites. "Only when the lesson of racial estrangement is learned," Toni Morrison reminds us, "is assimilation complete."[19]

Growing numbers of middle-class Mexican Americans thus made Faustian bargains that offered them inclusion within whiteness provided that they subsumed their ethnic identities under their newly acquired White racial identity and its core value of White supremacy. . . .

Not all Mexican Americans, of course, sought to define themselves as Caucasian or to achieve equality with Anglos on "the backs of blacks." One member of the Mexican American generation who resisted the lure of whiteness was Emma Tenayuca, a labor organizer and leader of the Pecan

Shellers Strike in San Antonio, Texas, during the 1930s. As a woman Tenayuca defied the gendered boundaries of both Anglo and Mexican culture when she assumed the role of labor activist; she also crossed the ideological divide between "patriotic Americans" and "traitors" when she joined the Communist Party.[20] While Anglos probably regarded Tenayuca as a stereotypical Mexican who had suddenly gone "loca," the largely Catholic, anti-Communist, and middle-class Mexican American community of San Antonio, which included LULAC leaders and the Catholic Church, opposed Tenayuca along ethnoracial fault lines as well as those of religion, gender, and politics. Tenayuca identified herself as an "Indian" like her father and was fond of saying that she did not have a "fashionable Spanish name like García or Sánchez."[21]

Despite numerous examples of those who, like Emma Tenayuca, rejected whiteness and White privilege, many Mexican Americans must nevertheless acknowledge their complicity in maintaining boundaries around "blackness" in order to claim the privileges of whiteness. By embracing whiteness, Mexican Americans have reinforced the color line that has denied people of African descent full participation in American democracy. In pursuing White rights, Mexican Americans combined Latin American racialism with Anglo racism, and in the process separated themselves and their political agenda from the Black civil rights struggles of the forties and fifties.

After 1960 a new generation of Mexican Americans, Chicanos and Chicanas, rejected the accommodationist strategies of the Mexican American generation and sought empowerment through "brownness" and the return, symbolically at least, to Aztlán, the heritage of their Indian past. Chicanos, many who were themselves middle class and college educated, were ridiculed for wearing serapes and resurrecting their Indian heritage, about which they knew very little, but these criticisms have largely missed the mark: in rejecting whiteness, Chicanos found common cause with all oppressed groups—Blacks, Indians, Chinese, and Vietnamese, as well as Mexican immigrants. They rejected the "wages of whiteness" as the "wages of sin" and celebrated their exclusion from and opposition to White America. The White response, about 150 years too late, was: "Why do you insist on being different, on being Chicano or Mexican? Why can't you just be American?" Chicanos rejected being "American" on the historically accurate grounds that being American had always meant being White. But as they accused LULAC members and conservative Mexican Americans of running from their brownness, it was also the case that many Chicanos were trying to escape from their whiteness. Many still are.

Today many Hispanics enjoy the "wages of whiteness" as a result of a complex matrix of phenotype, class position, culture, and citizenship status, as well as the willingness of many Anglos to make room for yet another group of off-white Hispanics. Still, many persons of Mexican descent, especially recent immigrants, are excluded from the domain of whiteness. A dark-skinned non-English-speaking Mexican immigrant doing lawn and garden work does not share the same class and ethnoracial status as acculturated, educated Hispanics. Hispanicized Mexican Americans themselves often construct a "racial" gulf between themselves and "illegal aliens" and "wetbacks."

The lure of whiteness continues to divide various Mexican constituencies along both race and class lines in their fractured, and often fractious, struggles for civil rights. Research on the various paths by which Mexican Americans sought to achieve their own civil rights goals since World War II has the potential to alter significantly our understanding of the complexity and confusion surrounding the ethnoracial identity of Mexican Americans and the process by which many became Hispanic, an identity given official sanction by the U.S. government, business, and academic communities. By examining how law (naturalization, segregation, and miscegenation), comparative civil rights politics (e.g., LULAC and NAACP), labor disputes, culture (e.g., "hispanismo"), religion (e.g., evangelical Protestantism), and literary works have constructed whiteness, often in conflicting and contradictory ways, such a study can illuminate the peculiarly hybrid identities of Mexican Americans and explore the historical roots of the tension that exists between the Hispanic and African American communities, analogous to the tension that has developed between Jews and Blacks, in the context of these groups' particular orientations toward whiteness.

NOTES

1. *LULAC* News 1 (1932) and 4 (1937), LULAC Collection, Benson Latin American Collection, University of Texas at Austin; and Benjamín Márquez, *LU-LAC: The Evolution of a Mexican American Political Association* (Austin: University of Texas Press, 1993), 32–33.

2. Márquez, *LULAC,* 33.

3. Toni Morrison, "On the Backs of Blacks," *Time* 142 (Fall 1993): 57.

4. Quoted in *Off White: Readings on Race, Power, and Society,* ed. Michelle Fine et al. (New York and London: Routledge, 1997), vii.

5. Mary Waters, *Ethnic Options: Choosing Identities in America* (Berkeley: University of California Press, 1990), 162.

6. George Lipsitz, "The Possessive Investment in Whiteness: Racialized Social Democracy and the 'White' Problem in American Studies," *American Quarterly* 47 (September 1995): 369–387. For the historical literature on whiteness, see David Roediger, *The Wages of Whiteness: Race and the Making of the American Working Class* (London: Verso, 1991); and his *Towards the Abolition of Whiteness: Essays on Race, Politics, and Working Class History* (London: Verso, 1994); Eric Lott, *Love and Theft: Blackface Minstrelsy and the American Working Class* (New York: Oxford University Press, 1993); Theodore W. Allen, *The Invention of the White Race,* vol. 1: *Racial Oppression and Social Control* (London: Verso, 1994); Alexander Saxton, *The Rise and Fall of the White Republic: Class Politics and Mass Culture in Nineteenth-Century America* (London: Verso, 1990); and Neil Foley, *The White Scourge: Mexicans, Blacks, and Poor*

Whites in Texas Cotton Culture (Berkeley: University of California Press, 1997). On the legal construction of whiteness, see Ian F. Haney López, *White by Law: The Legal Construction of Race* (New York: New York University Press, 1996); and Cheryl I. Harris, "Whiteness as Property," *Harvard Law Review* 106 (June 1993): 1709–1771. On racial formation and the gendered construction of racial ideologies, see Howard Winant, *Racial Conditions: Politics, Theory, Comparisons* (Minneapolis: University of Minnesota Press, 1994); Evelyn Brooks Higginbotham, "African-American Women's History and the Metalanguage of Race," *Signs* 17 (Winter 1992): 251–274; Peggy Pascoe, "Miscegenation Law, Court Cases, and Ideologies of 'Race' in Twentieth-Century America," *Journal of American History* 83 (June 1996): 44–69; Ruth Frankenberg, *White Women, Race Matters: The Social Construction of Whiteness* (Minneapolis: University of Minnesota Press, 1993); and Vron Ware, *Beyond the Pale: White Women, Racism, and History* (London: Verso, 1992). See also Barbara J. Fields, "Ideology and Race in America," in *Region, Race, and Reconstruction: Essays in Honor of C. Vann Woodward*, ed. J. Morgan Kousser and James M. McPherson (New York: Oxford University Press, 1982), 143–177; Thomas C. Holt, "Marking: Race, Race-Making, and the Writing of History," *American Historical Review* 100 (February 1995), 1–20; Toni Morrison, *Playing in the Dark: Whiteness and the Literary Imagination* (New York: Vintage Books, 1993); and Ronald Takaki, *Iron Cages: Race and Culture in 19th-Century America* (Seattle: University of Washington Press, 1979).

   7. Morrison, "On the Backs of Blacks," 57.

   8. Douglas R. Cope, *The Limits of Racial Domination in Mexico: Plebeian Society in Colonial Mexico City, 1600–1720* (Madison: University of Wisconsin Press, 1994); and Patricia Seed, "Social Dimensions of Race: Mexico City, 1753," *Hispanic American Historical Review* 62 (1982): 559–606. See also Michael C. Meyer and William L. Sherman, *The Course of Mexican History*, 5th ed. (New York: Oxford University Press, 1995), 214–215; and Magnus Mörner, *Race Mixture in the History of Latin America* (Boston: Little, Brown, 1967), 9–19.

   9. Raúl G. Domínguez to J. B. Davis, June 1, 1933, folder "Mexican Affairs," box 301–495, Miriam A. Ferguson Papers, Archives Division, Texas State Library, Austin, Texas. In another case the Mexican consul general in San Antonio wrote to the governor of Texas to protest the policy of Brackenridge Hospital in Austin, where Mexicans "are placed in the same ward with colored people, and treated as such." Ricardo G. Hill to James V. Allred, May 13, 1937, folder "Mexican Affairs," box 4-14/260, James Allred Papers, Texas State Library.

   10. José Vasconcelos, *The Cosmic Race* (1925; reprint, Baltimore: Johns Hopkins University Press, 1997); Madison Grant, *The Passing of the Great Race, Or the Racial Basis of European History* (New York: Charles Scribner's Sons, 1916), 69, 81; and C. M. Goethe, "Peons Need Not Apply," *World's Work* 59 (November 1930): 47–48.

   11. See Haney López, *White by Law;* and Harris, "Whiteness as Property."

   12. Haney López, *White by Law,* 89.

   13. The debate can be traced through the numerous congressional hearings by the Immigration and Naturalization Committee during the 1920s. See, for example, United States Congress, House, Committee on Immigration and Naturalization, *Immigration from Countries of the Western Hemisphere,* 70th Cong., 2nd sess. 1930;

idem, *Immigration from Countries of the Western Hemisphere,* 70th Cong., 1st scss., Hearing No. 70.1.5 (Washington, D.C.: Government Printing Office, 1928); idem, *Immigration from Mexico,* 71st Cong., 2nd sess. 1930; idem, *Naturalization,* 71st Cong., 2nd sess. 1930; idem, *Restriction of Immigration,* 68th Cong., 1st sess., serial 1-A. 1924; idem, *Seasonal Agricultural Laborers from Mexico,* 69th Cong., 1st sess. 1926; idem, *Temporary Admission of Illiterate Mexican Laborers,* 66th Cong., 2nd sess. 1920; idem, *Western Hemisphere Immigration,* 71st Cong., 2nd sess. 1930. For a scholarly treatment and analysis of the immigration debate, see Mark Reisler, *By the Sweat of Their Brow; Mexican Immigrant Labor in the United States, 1900–1940* (Westport, Conn.: Greenwood Press, 1976); and David G. Gutiérrez, ed., *Between Two Worlds. Mexican Immigrants in the United States* (Wilmington, Del.: Scholarly Resources, 1996).

14. Quoted in Gary A. Greenfield and Don B. Kates Jr., "Mexican Americans, Racial Discrimination, and the Civil Rights Act of 1866," *California Law Reveiw* 63 (January 1975), 700.

15. T. J. Woofter, Jr., *Races and Ethnic Groups in American Life* (New York: McGraw-Hill, 1933), 57; Greenfield and Kates, "Mexican Americans and the Civil Rights Act of 1866," *California Law Review* 63 (January 1975), 700.

16. Jorge C. Rangel and Carlos M. Alcalá, "Project Report: De Jure Segregation of Chicanos in Texas Schools," *Harvard Civil Rights–Civil Liberties Law Review* 7 (March 1972), 311–312, 332–333; Greenfield and Kates, "Mexican Americans and the Civil Rights Act of 1866," 682.

17. Quoted in Rangel and Alcalá, "De Jure Segregation of Chicanos in Texas Schools," 334. See also Guadalupe San Miguel, Jr., *"Let All of Them Take Heed": Mexican Americans and the Campaign for Educational Equality in Texas, 1910–1981* (Austin: University of Texas Press, 1987), 78–81.

18. Morrison, "On the Backs of Blacks," 57.

19. Morrison, "On the Backs of Blacks," 57.

20. Teresa Córdova et al., eds., *Chicana Voices: Intersections of Class, Race, and Gender* (Austin: Center for Mexican American Studies Publications, University of Texas at Austin, 1986), 38. See also Zaragosa Vargas, "Tejana Radical: Emma Tenayuca and the San Antonio Labor Movement," *Pacific Historical Review* (1997).

21. Córdova, *Chicana Voices,* 38.

chapter**six**

The Possessive Investment in Whiteness

–George Lipsitz

> *Blacks are often confronted, in American life, with such devastating examples of the white descent from dignity; devastating not only because of the enormity of white pretensions, but because this swift and graceless descent would seem to indicate that white people have no principles whatever.*
>
> **—James Baldwin**

Shortly after World War II, a French reporter asked expatriate Richard Wright for his views about the "Negro problem" in America. The author replied, "There isn't any Negro problem; there is only a white problem."[1] By inverting the reporter's question, Wright called attention to its hidden assumptions—that racial polarization comes from the existence of blacks rather than from the behavior of whites, that black people are a "problem" for whites rather than fellow citizens entitled to justice, and that, unless otherwise specified, "Americans" means "whites."[2] But Wright's formulation also placed political mobilization by African Americans during the civil rights era in context, connecting black disadvantages to white advantages and finding the roots of black consciousness in the systemic practices of aversion, exploitation, denigration, and discrimination practiced by people who think of themselves as "white."

Whiteness is everywhere in U.S. culture, but it is very hard to see. As Richard Dyer suggests, "[W]hite power secures its dominance by seeming not to be anything in particular."[3] As the unmarked category against which difference is constructed, whiteness never has to speak its name, never has to acknowledge its role as an organizing principle in social and cultural relations.[4] To identify, analyze, and oppose the destructive consequences of whiteness, we need what Walter Benjamin called "presence of mind." Benjamin wrote that people visit fortune-tellers less out of a desire to know the future than out of a fear of not noticing some important aspect of the present. "Presence of mind," he suggested, "is an abstract of the future, and precise awareness of the present moment more decisive than foreknowledge of the most distant events."[5] In U.S. society at this time, precise awareness of the present moment requires an understanding of the existence and the destructive consequences of the possessive investment in whiteness that surreptitiously shapes so much of our public and private lives."

Race is a cultural construct, but one with sinister structural causes and consequences. Conscious and deliberate actions have institutionalized group identity in the United States, not just through the dissemination of cultural stories, but also through systematic efforts from colonial times to the present to create economic advantages through a possessive investment in whiteness for European Americans. Studies of culture too far removed from studies of social structure leave us with inadequate explanations for understanding racism and inadequate remedies for combating it.

Desire for slave labor encouraged European settlers in North America to view, first, Native Americans and, later, African Americans as racially inferior people suited "by nature" for the humiliating subordination of involuntary servitude. The long history of the possessive investment in whiteness stems in no small measure from the fact that all subsequent immigrants to North America have come to an already racialized society. From the start, European settlers in North America established structures encouraging a possessive investment in whiteness. The colonial and early national legal systems authorized attacks on Native Americans and encouraged the appropriation of their lands. They legitimated racialized chattel slavery, limited naturalized citizenship to "white" immigrants, identified Asian immigrants as expressly unwelcome (through legislation aimed at immigrants from China in 1882, from India in 1917, from Japan in 1924, and from the Philippines in 1934), and provided pretexts for restricting the voting, exploiting the labor, and seizing the property of Asian Americans, Mexican Americans, Native Americans, and African Americans.[6]

The possessive investment in whiteness is not a simple matter of black and white; all racialized minority groups have suffered from it, albeit to different degrees and in different ways. The African slave trade began in earnest only after large-scale Native American slavery proved impractical in North America. The abolition of slavery led to the importation of low-wage labor from Asia. Legislation banning immigration from Asia set the stage for the recruitment of low-wage labor from Mexico. The new racial categories that emerged in each of these eras all revolved around applying racial labels to "nonwhite" groups in order to stigmatize and exploit them while at the same time preserving the value of whiteness.

Although reproduced in new form in every era, the possessive investment in whiteness has always been influenced by its origins in the racialized history of the United States — by its legacy of slavery and segregation, of "Indian" extermination and immigrant restriction, of conquest and colonialism. Although slavery has existed in many countries without any particular racial dimensions to it, the slave system that emerged in North America soon took on distinctly racial forms. Africans enslaved in North America faced a racialized system of power that reserved permanent, hereditary, chattel slavery for black people. White settlers institutionalized a possessive investment in whiteness by making blackness synonymous with slavery and whiteness synonymous with freedom, but also by pitting people of color against one another. Fearful of alliances between Native Americans and African Americans that might challenge the prerogatives of whiteness, white settlers prohibited slaves and free blacks from traveling in "Indian country." European Americans used diplomacy and force to compel Native Americans to return runaway slaves to their white masters. During the Stono Rebellion of 1739, colonial authorities offered Native Americans a bounty for every rebellious slave they captured or killed. At the same time, British settlers recruited black slaves to fight against Native Americans within colonial militias.[7] The power of whiteness depended not only on white hegemony over separate racialized groups, but also on manipulating racial outsiders to fight against one another, to compete with each other for white approval, and to seek the rewards and privileges of whiteness for themselves at the expense of other racialized populations. . . .

Yet today the possessive investment is not simply the residue of conquest and colonialism, of slavery and segregation, of immigrant exclusion and "Indian" extermination. Contemporary whiteness and its rewards have been created and recreated by policies adopted long after the emancipation of slaves in the 1860s and even after the outlawing of *de jure* segregation in the 1960s. There has always been racism in the United States, but it has not always been the same racism. Political and cultural struggles over power have shaped the contours and dimensions of racism differently in different eras. . . .

Contemporary racism has been created anew in many ways over the past five decades, but most dramatically by the putatively race-neutral, liberal, social democratic reforms of the New Deal Era and by the more overtly race-conscious neoconservative reactions against liberalism since the Nixon years. It is a mistake to posit a gradual and inevitable trajectory of evolutionary progress in race relations; on the contrary, our history shows that battles won at one moment can later be lost. Despite hard-fought battles for change that secured important concessions during the

1960s in the form of civil rights legislation, the racialized nature of social policy in the United States since the Great Depression has actually increased the possessive investment in whiteness among European Americans over the past half century.

During the New Deal Era of the 1930s and 1940s, both the Wagner Act and the Social Security Act excluded farm workers and domestics from coverage, effectively denying those disproportionately minority sectors of the work force protections and benefits routinely afforded whites. The Federal Housing Act of 1934 brought home ownership within reach of millions of citizens by placing the credit of the federal government behind private lending to home buyers, but overtly racist categories in the Federal Housing Agency's (FHA) "confidential" city surveys and appraisers' manuals channeled almost all of the loan money toward whites and away from communities of color.[8] In the post-World War II era, trade unions negotiated contract provisions giving private medical insurance, pensions, and job security largely to the white workers who formed the overwhelming majority of the unionized work force in mass production industries, rather than fighting for full employment, medical care, and old-age pensions for all, or even for an end to discriminatory hiring and promotion practices by employers in those industries.[9]

Each of these policies widened the gap between the resources available to whites and those available to aggrieved racial communities. Federal housing policy offers an important illustration of the broader principles at work in the possessive investment in whiteness. By channeling loans away from older inner-city neighborhoods and toward white home buyers moving into segregated suburbs, the FHA and private lenders after World War II aided and abetted segregation in U.S. residential neighborhoods. FHA appraisers denied federally supported loans to prospective home buyers in the racially mixed Boyle Heights neighborhood of Los Angeles in 1939, for example, because the area struck them as a "'melting pot' area literally honeycombed with diverse and subversive racial elements."[10] Similarly, mostly white St. Louis County secured five times as many FHA mortgages as the more racially mixed city of St. Louis between 1943 and 1960. Home buyers in the county received six times as much loan money and enjoyed per capita mortgage spending 6.3 times greater than those in the city.[11]

The federal government has played a major role in augmenting the possessive investment in whiteness. For years, the General Services Administration routinely channeled the government's own rental and leasing business to realtors who engaged in racial discrimination, while federally subsidized urban renewal plans reduced the already limited supply of housing for communities of color through "slum clearance" programs. In concert with FHA support for segregation in the suburbs, federal and state tax monies routinely funded the construction of water supplies and sewage facilities for racially exclusive suburban communities in the 1940s and 1950s. By the 1960s, these areas often incorporated themselves as independent municipalities in order to gain greater access to federal funds allocated for "urban aid."[12]

At the same time that FHA loans and federal highway building projects subsidized the growth of segregated suburbs, urban renewal programs in cities throughout the country devastated minority neighborhoods. During the 1950s and 1960s, federally assisted urban renewal projects destroyed 20 percent of the central-city housing units occupied by blacks, as opposed to only 10 percent of those inhabited by whites.[13] More than 60 percent of those displaced by urban renewal were African Americans, Puerto Ricans, Mexican Americans, or members of other minority racial groups.[14] The Federal Housing Administration and the Veterans Administration financed more than $120 billion worth of new housing between 1934 and 1962, but less than 2 percent of this real estate was available to nonwhite families—and most of that small amount was located in segregated areas.[15]

Even in the 1970s, after most major urban renewal programs had been completed, black central-city residents continued to lose housing units at a rate equal to 80 percent of what had been lost in the 1960s. Yet white displacement declined to the relatively low levels of the 1950s.[16] In addition, the refusal first to pass, then to enforce, fair housing laws has enabled realtors, buyers, and sellers to profit from racist collusion against minorities largely without fear of legal retribution. During the decades following World War II, urban renewal helped construct a new "white" identity in the suburbs by helping to destroy ethnically specific European American urban inner-city neighborhoods. Wrecking balls and bulldozers eliminated some of these sites, while others were transformed by an influx of minority residents desperately competing for a declining supply of affordable housing units. As increasing numbers of racial minorities moved into cities, increasing numbers of European American ethnics moved out. Consequently, ethnic differences among whites became a less important dividing line in U.S. culture, while race became more important. The suburbs helped turn Euro-Americans into "whites" who could live near each other and intermarry with relatively little difficulty. But this "white" unity rested on residential segregation, on shared access to housing and life chances largely unavailable to communities of color.[17]

During the 1950s and 1960s, local "pro-growth" coalitions led by liberal mayors often justified urban renewal as a program designed to build more housing for poor people, but it actually destroyed more housing than it created. Ninety percent of the low-income units removed for urban renewal during the entire history of the program were never replaced. Commercial, industrial, and municipal projects occupied more than 80 percent of the land cleared for these projects, with less than 20 percent allocated for replacement housing. In addition, the loss of taxable properties and the tax abatements granted to new enterprises in urban renewal zones often meant serious tax increases for poor, working-class, and middle-class home owners and renters.[18] Although the percentage of black suburban dwellers also increased during this period, no significant desegregation of the suburbs took place. From 1960 to 1977, 4 million whites moved out of central cities, while the number of whites living in suburbs increased by 22 million; during the same years, the inner-city black population grew by 6 million, but the number of blacks living in suburbs increased by only 500,000.[19] By 1993, 86 percent of suburban whites still lived in places with a black population below 1 percent. At the same time, cities with large numbers of minority residents found themselves cut off from loans by the FHA. For example, because of their growing black and Puerto Rican populations, neither Camden nor Paterson, New Jersey, in 1966 received one FHA-sponsored mortgage.[20]

In 1968, lobbyists for the banking industry helped draft the Housing and Urban Development Act, which allowed private lenders to shift the risks of financing low-income housing to the government, creating a lucrative and thoroughly unregulated market for themselves. One section of the 1968 bill authorized FHA mortgages for inner-city areas that did not meet the usual eligibility criteria, and another section subsidized interest payments by low-income families. If administered wisely, these provisions might have promoted fair housing goals, but FHA administrators deployed them in ways that actually promoted segregation in order to provide banks, brokers, lenders, developers, realtors, and speculators with windfall profits. As a U.S. Commission on Civil Rights investigation later revealed, FHA officials collaborated with blockbusters in financing the flight of low-income whites out of inner-city neighborhoods, and then aided unscrupulous realtors and speculators by arranging purchases of substandard housing by minorities desperate to own their own homes. The resulting sales and mortgage foreclosures brought great profits to lenders (almost all of them white), but their actions led to price fixing and a subsequent inflation of housing costs in the inner city by more than 200 percent between 1968 and 1972. Bankers then foreclosed on the mortgages of thousands of these uninspected and substandard homes, ruining many inner-city neighborhoods. In response, the Department of Housing and Urban Development essentially red-lined inner cities, making them ineligible for future loans, a decision that destroyed the value of inner-city housing for generations to come.[21]

Federally funded highways designed to connect suburban commuters with downtown places of employment also destroyed already scarce housing in minority communities and often disrupted neighborhood life as well. Construction of the Harbor Freeway in Los Angeles, the Gulf Freeway in Houston, and the Mark Twain Freeway in St. Louis displaced thousands of residents and bisected neighborhoods, shopping districts, and political precincts. The processes of urban renewal and highway construction set in motion a vicious cycle: population loss led to decreased political power, which made minority neighborhoods more vulnerable to further urban renewal and freeway construction, not to mention more susceptible to the placement of prisons, incinerators, toxic waste dumps, and other projects that further depopulated these areas.

In Houston, Texas—where blacks make up slightly more than one quarter of the local population—more than 75 percent of municipal garbage incinerators and 100 percent of the city-owned garbage dumps are located in black neighborhoods.[22] A 1992 study by staff writers for the *National Law Journal* examined the Environmental Protection Agency's response to 1,177 toxic waste cases and found that polluters of sites near the greatest white population received penalties 500 percent higher than penalties imposed on polluters in minority areas—an average of $335,566 for white areas contrasted with $55,318 for minority areas. Income did not account for these differences—penalties for low-income areas on average actually exceeded those for areas with the highest median incomes by about 3 percent. The penalties for violating all federal environmental laws regulating air, water, and waste pollution were 46 percent lower in minority communities than in white communities. In addition, superfund remedies left minority communities waiting longer than white communities to be placed on the national priority list, cleanups that began from 12 to 42 percent later than at white sites, and with a 7 percent greater likelihood of "containment" (walling off a hazardous site) than cleanup, while white sites experienced treatment and cleanup 22 percent more often than containment.[23]

The federal Agency for Toxic Substances and Disease Registry's 1988 survey of children suffering from lead poisoning showed that among families with incomes under $6,000 per year, 36 percent of white children but 68 percent of black children suffered from excess lead in their bloodstreams. Among families with incomes above $15,000 per year, only 12 percent of white children but 38 percent of black children suffered from toxic levels of lead.[24] In the Los Angeles area, only 34 percent of whites inhabit areas with the most polluted air, but 71 percent of African Americans and 50 percent of Latinos live in neighborhoods with the highest levels of air pollution.[25] Nationwide, 60 percent of African Americans and Latinos live in communities with uncontrolled toxic waste sites.[26]

Scholarly studies reveal that even when adjusted for income, education, and occupational status, aggrieved racial minorities encounter higher levels of exposure to toxic substances than white people experience.[27] In 1987, the Commission for Racial Justice of the United Church of Christ found race to be the most significant variable in determining the location of commercial hazardous waste facilities.[28] In a review of sixty-four studies examining environmental disparities, the National Wildlife Federation found that racial disparities outnumbered disparities by income, and in cases where disparities in race and income were both present, race proved to be more important in twenty-two out of thirty tests.[29] As Robert D.

Bullard demonstrates, "race has been found to be an independent factor, not reducible to class" in predicting exposure to a broad range of environmental hazards, including polluted air, contaminated fish, lead poisoning, municipal landfills, incinerators, and toxic waste dumps.[30] The combination of exposure to environmental hazards and employment discrimination establishes a sinister correlation between race and health. One recent government study revealed that the likelihood of dying from nutritional deficiencies was two and a half times greater among African Americans than among European Americans.[31] Another demonstrated that Asian and Pacific Islander recipients of aid for at-risk families exhibited alarming rates of stunted growth and underweight among children under the age of five.[32] Corporations systematically target Native American reservations when looking for locations for hazardous waste incinerators, solid waste landfills, and nuclear waste storage facilities; Navajo teenagers develop reproductive organ cancer at seventeen times the national average because of their exposure to radiation from uranium mines."[33] Latinos in East Los Angeles encounter some of the worst smog and the highest concentration of air toxins in southern California because of prevailing wind patterns and the concentration of polluting industries, freeways, and toxic waste dumps.[34] Environmental racism makes the possessive investment in whiteness literally a matter of life and death; if African Americans had access to the nutrition, wealth, health care, and protection against environmental hazards offered routinely to whites, seventy-five thousand fewer of them would die each year.[35]

Minorities are less likely than whites to receive preventive medical care or costly operations from Medicare. Eligible members of minority communities are also less likely than European Americans to apply for food stamps.[36] The labor of migrant farm workers from aggrieved racialized groups plays a vital role in providing adequate nutrition for others, but the farm workers and their children suffer disproportionately from health disorders caused by malnutrition.[37] In her important research on health policy and ethnic diversity, Linda Wray concludes that "the lower life expectancies for many ethnic minority groups and subgroups stem largely from their disproportionately higher rates of poverty, malnutrition, and poor health care."[38]

Just as residential segregation and urban renewal make minority communities disproportionately susceptible to health hazards, their physical and social location gives these communities a different relationship to the criminal justice system. A 1990 study by the National Institute on Drug Abuse revealed that while only 15 percent of the thirteen million habitual drug users in the United States were black and 77 percent were white, African Americans were four times more likely to be arrested on drug charges than whites in the nation as a whole, and seven to nine times more likely in Pennsylvania, Michigan, Illinois, Florida, Massachusetts, and New Jersey. A 1989 study by the Parents' Resource Institute for Drug Education discovered that African American high school students consistently showed lower levels of drug and alcohol use than their European American counterparts, even in high schools populated by residents of low-income housing projects. Yet, while comprising about 12 percent of the U.S. population, blacks accounted for 10 percent of drug arrests in 1984, 40 percent in 1988, and 42 percent in 1990. In addition, white drug defendants receive considerably shorter average prison terms than African Americans convicted of comparable crimes. A U.S. Sentencing Commission study found in 1992 that half of the federal court districts that handled cases involving crack cocaine prosecuted minority defendants *exclusively*. A *Los Angeles Times* article in 1995 revealed that "black and Latino crack dealers are hammered with 10-year mandatory federal sentences while whites prosecuted in state court face a minimum of five years and often receive no more than a year in jail." Alexander Lichtenstein and Michael A. Kroll point out that sentences for African Americans in the federal prison system are 20 percent longer than those given to whites who commit the same crimes. They observe that if blacks received the same sentences as whites for these offenses, the federal prison system would require three thousand fewer prison cells, enough to close completely six of the new five-hundred bed institutions.[39]

Racial animus on the part of police officers, prosecutors, and judges accounts for only a small portion of the distinctive experience that racial minorities have with the criminal justice system. Economic devastation makes the drug trade appealing to some people in the inner city, while the dearth of capital in minority neighborhoods curtails opportunities for other kinds of employment. Deindustrialization, unemployment, and lack of intergenerational transfers of wealth undermine parental and adult authority in many neighborhoods. The complex factors that cause people to turn to drugs are no more prevalent in minority communities than elsewhere, but these communities and their inhabitants face more stress while having fewer opportunities to receive private counseling and treatment for their problems.

The structural weaknesses of minority neighborhoods caused by discrimination in housing, education, and hiring also play a crucial role in relations between inner-city residents and the criminal justice system. Cocaine dealing, which initially skyrocketed among white suburban residents, was driven into the inner city by escalating enforcement pressures in wealthy white communities. Ghettos and barrios became distribution centers for the sale of drugs to white suburbanites. Former New York and Houston police commissioner Lee Brown, head of the federal government's antidrug efforts during the early years of the Clinton presidency and later mayor of Houston, noted, "There are those who bring drugs into the country. That's not the black community. Then you have wholesalers, those who distribute them once they get here, and as a rule that's not the black community. Where you find the blacks is in the street dealing."[40]

You also find blacks and other minorities in prison. Police officers in large cities, pressured to show results in the drive against drugs, lack the resources to effectively enforce the law everywhere (in part because of the social costs of deindustrialization and the tax limitation initiatives designed to shrink the size of government). These officers know that it is easier to make arrests and to secure convictions by confronting drug users in areas that have conspicuous street corner sales, that have more people out on the street with no place to go, and that have residents more likely to plead guilty and less likely to secure the services of attorneys who can get the charges against them dropped, reduced, or wiped off the books with subsequent successful counseling and rehabilitation. In addition, politicians supported by the public relations efforts of neoconservative foundations often portray themselves to suburban voters as opponents of the "dangerous classes" in the inner cities.

Minority disadvantages craft advantages for others. Urban renewal failed to provide new housing for the poor, but it played an important role in transforming the U.S. urban economy from one that relied on factory production to one driven by producer services. Urban renewal projects subsidized the development of downtown office centers on previously residential land, and they frequently created buffer zones of empty blocks dividing poor neighborhoods from new shopping centers designed for affluent commuters. To help cities compete for corporate investment by making them appealing to high-level executives, federal urban aid favored construction of luxury housing units and cultural centers like symphony halls and art museums over affordable housing for workers. Tax abatements granted to these producer services centers further aggravated the fiscal crisis that cities faced, leading to tax increases on existing industries, businesses, and residences.

Workers from aggrieved racial minorities bore the brunt of this transformation. Because the 1964 Civil Rights Act came so late, minority workers who received jobs because of it found themselves more vulnerable to seniority-based layoffs when businesses automated or transferred operations overseas. Although the act initially made real progress in reducing employment discrimination, lessened the gaps between rich and poor and between black and white workers, and helped bring minority poverty to its lowest level in history in 1973, that year's recession initiated a reversal of minority progress and a reassertion of white privilege.[41] In 1977, the U.S. Civil Rights Commission reported on the disproportionate impact of layoffs on minority workers. In cases where minority workers made up only 10 to 12 percent of the work force in their area, they accounted for from 60 to 70 percent of those laid off in 1974. The principle of seniority, a trade union triumph designed to protect workers from age discrimination, in this case guaranteed that minority workers would suffer most from technological changes, because the legacy of past discrimination by their employers left them with less seniority than white workers.[42]

When housing prices increased dramatically during the 1970s, white home owners who had been able to take advantage of discriminatory FHA financing policies in the past realized increased equity in their homes, while those excluded from the housing market by earlier policies found themselves facing even higher costs of entry into the market in addition to the traditional obstacles presented by the discriminatory practices of sellers, realtors, and lenders. The contrast between European Americans and African Americans is instructive in this regard. Because whites have access to broader housing choices than blacks, whites pay 15 percent less than blacks for similar housing in the same neighborhood. White neighborhoods typically experience housing costs 25 percent lower than would be the case if the residents were black.[43]

A recent Federal Reserve Bank of Boston study revealed that Boston bankers made 2.9 times as many mortgage loans per 1,000 housing units in neighborhoods inhabited by low-income whites than in neighborhoods populated by low-income blacks.[44] In addition, loan officers were far more likely to overlook flaws in the credit records of white applicants or to arrange creative financing for them than they were with black applicants.[45] A Los Angeles study found that loan officers more frequently used dividend income and underlying assets as criteria for judging black applicants than for whites.[46] In Houston, the NCNB Bank of Texas disqualified 13 percent of middle-income white loan applicants but 36 percent of middle-income black applicants.[47] Atlanta's home loan institutions gave five times as many home loans to whites as to blacks in the late 1980s. An analysis of sixteen Atlanta neighborhoods found that home buyers in white neighborhoods received conventional financing four times as often as those in black sections of the city.[48] Nationwide, financial institutions receive more money in deposits from black neighborhoods than they invest in them in the form of home mortgage loans, making home lending a vehicle for the transfer of capital away from black savers toward white investors.[49] In many locations, high-income blacks were denied loans more often than low-income whites.[50]

When confronted with evidence of systematic racial bias in home lending, defenders of the possessive investment in whiteness argue that the disproportionate share of loan denials to members of minority groups stems not from discrimination, but from the low net worth of minority applicants, even those who have high incomes. This might seem a reasonable position, but net worth is almost totally determined by past opportunities for asset accumulation, and therefore is the one figure most likely to reflect the history of discrimination. Minorities are told, in essence, "We can't give you a loan today because we've discriminated against members of your race so effectively in the past that you have not been able to accumulate any equity from housing and to pass it down through the generations."

Most white families have acquired their net worth from the appreciation of property that they secured under conditions of special privilege in a discriminatory housing market. In their prize-winning book *Black Wealth/White Wealth*, Melvin Oliver and Thomas Shapiro demonstrate how the history of housing discrimination makes white parents more able to borrow funds for their children's college education or to loan money to their children to enter the housing market. In addition, much discrimination in home lending is not based on considerations of net worth; it stems from decisions made by white banking officials based on their stereotypes about minority communities. The Federal Reserve Bank of Boston study showed that black and Latino mortgage applicants are 60 percent more likely to be turned down for loans than whites, even after controlling for employment, financial, and neighborhood characteristics.[51] Ellis Cose reports on a white bank official confronted with evidence at a board of directors' meeting that his bank denied loans to blacks who had credit histories and earnings equal to those of white applicants who received loans. The banker replied that the information indicated that the bank needed to do a better job of "affirmative action," but one of his colleagues pointed out that the problem had nothing to do with affirmative action— the bank was simply letting prejudice stand in the way of its own best interests by rejecting loans that should be approved.[52]

Yet bankers also make money from the ways in which discrimination creates artificial scarcities in the market. Minorities have to pay more for housing because much of the market is off limits to them. Blockbusters profit from exploiting white fears and provoking them into panic selling. Minority home owners denied loans in mainstream banks often turn to exploitative lenders who make "low end" loans at enormously high interest rates. If they fail to pay back these loans, regular banks can acquire the property cheaply and charge someone else exorbitant interest for a loan on the same property.

Federal home loan policies have put the power of the federal government at the service of private discrimination. Urban renewal and highway construction programs have enhanced the possessive investment in whiteness directly through government initiatives. In addition, decisions about where to locate federal jobs have also systematically subsidized whiteness. Federal civilian employment dropped by 41,419 in central cities between 1966 and 1973, but total federal employment in metropolitan areas grew by 26,558.[53] While one might naturally expect the location of government buildings that serve the public to follow population trends, the federal government's policy of locating offices and records centers in suburbs aggravated the flight of jobs to suburban locations less accessible to inner-city residents. Because racial discrimination in the private sector forces minority workers to seek government positions disproportionate to their numbers, these moves exact particular hardships on them. In addition, minorities who follow their jobs to the suburbs must generally allocate more for commuter costs, because housing discrimination makes it harder and more expensive for them than for whites to relocate.

The policies of neoconservatives in the Reagan and Bush administrations during the 1980s and 1990s greatly exacerbated the racialized aspects of more than fifty years of these social welfare policies. Regressive policies that cut federal aid to education and refused to challenge segregated education, housing, and hiring, as well as the cynical cultivation of an antiblack consensus through attacks on affirmative action and voting rights legislation clearly reinforced possessive investments in whiteness. In the U.S. economy, where 86 percent of available jobs do not appear in classified ads and where personal connections prove the most important factor in securing employment, attacks on affirmative action guarantee that whites will be rewarded for their historical advantage in the labor market rather than for their individual abilities or efforts.[54]

Attacking the civil rights tradition serves many functions for neoconservatives. By mobilizing existing racisms and generating new ones, neoconservatives seek to discredit the egalitarian and democratic social movements of the post-World War II era and to connect the attacks by those movements on wealth, special privilege, and elite control over education and opportunity to despised and unworthy racial "others."

Attacks on the gains made by civil rights activism also act as a wedge to divide potentially progressive coalitions along racial lines, a strategy that attained its peak moment with the defection of "blue collar" trade unionists from the Democratic Party in the 1980s to become "Reagan Democrats." In addition to protecting centralized power and wealth and dividing its opponents, the neoracism of contemporary conservatism also functions as an important unifying symbol for a disparate and sometimes antagonistic coalition that includes Hamiltonian big-government conservatives as well as antistate libertarians, and that incorporates born-again Christians into an alliance with "objectivist" free market thinkers who celebrate selfishness and view the love of gain as the engine of human progress. This coalition often has trouble agreeing on the things it favors, but it has no difficulty agreeing about the alleged bad behavior and inferior morality of minority individuals and communities. Most important, by generating an ever repeating cycle of "moral panics" about the family, crime, welfare, race, and terrorism, neoconservatives produce a perpetual state of anxiety that obscures the actual failures of conservatism as economic and social policy, while promoting demands for even more draconian measures of a similar nature for the future. The neoracism of contemporary conservatism plays a vital role in building a countersubversive consensus because it disguises the social disintegration brought about by neoconservatism itself as the fault of "inferior" social groups, and because it builds a sense of righteous indignation among its constituents that enables them to believe that the selfish and self-interested politics they pursue are actually part of a moral crusade.

Yet even seemingly race-neutral policies supported by both neoconservatives and liberals in the 1980s and 1990s have increased the absolute value of being white. In the 1980s, changes in federal tax laws decreased the value of wage income and increased the value of investment income—a move harmful to minorities, who suffer from a gap between their total wealth and that of whites even greater than the disparity between their income and white income. The failure to raise the minimum wage between 1981 and

1989 and the decline of more than one-third in the value of Aid to Families with Dependent Children (AFDC) payments injured all poor people, but they exacted special costs on nonwhites, who faced even more constricted markets for employment, housing, and education than poor whites.[55]

Similarly, the "tax reforms" of the 1980s made the effective rate of taxation higher on investment in actual goods and services than on profits from speculative enterprises. This change encouraged the flight of capital from industrial production with its many employment opportunities toward investments that can be turned over quickly to allow the greatest possible tax write-offs. Government policies thus discouraged investments that might produce high-paying jobs and encouraged investors to strip companies of their assets to make rapid short-term profits. These policies hurt almost all workers, but they fell particularly heavily on minority workers, who because of employment discrimination in the retail and small business sectors were overrepresented in blue-collar industrial jobs.

On the other hand, while neoconservative tax policies created incentives for employers to move their enterprises elsewhere, they created disincentives for home owners to move. Measures like California's Proposition 13 (passed in 1978) granting tax relief to property owners badly misallocate housing resources, because they make it financially unwise for the elderly to move out of large houses, further reducing the supply of housing available to young families. While one can well understand the necessity for protecting senior citizens on fixed incomes from tax increases that would make them lose their homes, the rewards and punishments provided by Proposition 13 are so extreme that they prevent the kinds of generational succession that have routinely opened up housing to young families in the past. This reduction works particular hardships on those who also face discrimination by sellers, realtors, and lending institutions.

Subsidies to the private sector by government agencies also tend to enhance the rewards of past discrimination. Throughout the country, tax increment financing for redevelopment programs offers tax-free and low-interest loans to developers whose projects use public services, often without having to pay taxes to local school boards or county governments. In St. Louis, for example, tax abatements for wealthy corporations deprive the city's schools (and their majority African American population) of $17 million a year. Even if these redevelopment projects eventually succeed in increasing municipal revenues through sales and earnings taxes, their proceeds go to funds that pay for the increased services these developments demand (fire and police protection, roads, sewers, electricity, lighting, etc.) rather than to school funds, which are dependent upon property tax revenues.[56] Nationwide, industrial development bonds resulted in a $7.4 billion tax loss in 1983, which ordinary taxpayers had to make up through increased payroll taxes. Compared to white Americans, people of color, more likely to be poor or working class, suffer disproportionately from these changes as taxpayers, as workers, and as tenants. A study by the

Citizens for Tax Justice found that wealthy Californians spend less than eleven cents in taxes for every dollar earned, while poor residents of the state pay fourteen cents out of every dollar in taxes. As groups overrepresented among the poor, minorities have been forced to subsidize the tax breaks given to the wealthy.[57] While holding property tax assessments for businesses and some home owners to about half of their market value, California's Proposition 13 deprived cities and counties of $13 billion a year in taxes. Businesses alone avoided $3.3 billion to $8.6 billion in taxes per year under this statute.[58]

Because they are ignorant of even the recent history of the possessive investment in whiteness—generated by slavery and segregation, immigrant exclusion and Native American policy, conquest and colonialism, but augmented by liberal and conservative social policies as well—Americans produce largely cultural explanations for structural social problems. The increased possessive investment in whiteness generated by disinvestment in U.S. cities, factories, and schools since the 1970s disguises as *racial* problems the general social problems posed by deindustrialization, economic restructuring, and neoconservative attacks on the welfare state. It fuels a discourse that demonizes people of color for being victimized by these changes, while hiding the privileges of whiteness by attributing the economic advantages enjoyed by whites to their family values, faith in fatherhood, and foresight—rather than to the favoritism they enjoy through their possessive investment in whiteness.

The demonization of black families in public discourse since the 1970s is particularly instructive in this regard. During the 1970s, the share of low-income households headed by blacks increased by one-third, while black family income fell from 60 percent of white family income in 1971 to 58 percent in 1980. Even adjusting for unemployment and for African American disadvantages in life-cycle employment (more injuries, more frequently interrupted work histories, confinement to jobs most susceptible to layoffs), the wages of full-time year-round black workers fell from 77 percent of white workers' income to 73 percent by 1986. In 1986, white workers with high school diplomas earned $3,000 per year more than African Americans with the same education.[59] Even when they had the same family structure as white workers, blacks found themselves more likely to be poor.

Recent economic gains by blacks brighten the picture somewhat, but the deindustrialization and economic restructuring of the 1970s and 1980s imposes yet another racial penalty on wage earners from minority communities, who suffered setbacks while members of other groups accumulated equity-producing assets. And even when some minority groups show improvement, others do not. In 1995, for example, every U.S. ethnic and racial group experienced an increase in income except the twenty-seven million Hispanics, who experienced a 5.1 percent drop in income during that year alone.[60]

Forty-six percent of black workers between the ages of twenty and twenty-four held blue-collar jobs in 1976, but only 20 percent by 1984. Earnings by young black families that had reached 60 percent of white families' income in 1973, fell to 46 percent by 1986. Younger African American families experienced a 50 percent drop in real earnings between 1973 and 1986, with the decline in black male wages particularly steep.[61] Many recent popular and scholarly studies have delineated the causes for black economic decline over the past two decades.[62] Deindustrialization has decimated the industrial infrastructure that formerly provided high wage jobs and chances for upward mobility to black workers. Neoconservative attacks on government spending for public housing, health, education, and transportation have deprived members of minority groups of needed services and opportunities for jobs in the public sector. A massive retreat at the highest levels of government from the responsibility to enforce antidiscrimination laws has sanctioned pervasive overt and covert racial discrimination by bankers, realtors, and employers.

Yet public opinion polls of white Americans reflect little recognition of these devastating changes. Seventy percent of whites in one poll said that African Americans "have the same opportunities to live a middle-class life as whites," and nearly three-fourths of white respondents to a 1989 poll believed that opportunities for blacks had improved under Reagan.[63] If such optimism about the opportunities available to African Americans does not demonstrate ignorance of the dire conditions facing black communities, it indicates that many whites believe that blacks suffer deservedly, because they do not take advantage of the opportunities offered them. In opinion polls, favorable assessments of black chances for success often accompanied extremely negative judgments about the abilities, work habits, and character of black people. A National Opinion Research Report in 1990 disclosed that more than 50 percent of U.S. whites viewed blacks as innately lazy and less intelligent and less patriotic than whites.[64] More than 60 percent said that they believed that blacks suffer from poor housing and employment opportunities because of their own lack of will power. Some 56.3 percent said that blacks preferred welfare to employment, while 44.6 percent contended that blacks tended toward laziness.[65] Even more important, research by Mary Edsall and Thomas Byrne Edsall indicates that many whites structure nearly all of their decisions about housing, education, and politics in response to their aversions to black people.[66]

The present political culture in this country gives broad sanction for viewing white supremacy and antiblack racism as forces from the past, as demons finally put to rest by the passage of the 1964 Civil Rights Act and the 1965 Voting Rights Act.[67] Jurists, journalists, and politicians have generally been more vocal in opposing what they call "quotas" and "reverse discrimination"—by which they usually mean race-specific measures, designed to remedy existing racial discrimination, that inconvenience or offend whites—than in challenging the thousands of well-documented cases every year of routine, systematic, and unyielding discrimination against minorities. It is my contention that the stark contrast between non-white experiences and white opinions during the past two decades cannot be attributed solely to individual ignorance or intolerance, but stems instead from liberal individualism's inability to describe adequately the collective dimensions of our experience.[68] As long as we define social life as the sum total of conscious and deliberative individual activities, we will be able to discern as racist only *individual* manifestations of personal prejudice and hostility. Systemic, collective, and coordinated group behavior consequently drops out of sight. Collective exercises of power that relentlessly channel rewards, resources, and opportunities from one group to another will not appear "racist" from this perspective, because they rarely announce their intention to discriminate against individuals. Yet they nonetheless give racial identities their sinister social meaning by giving people from different races vastly different life chances.

The gap between white perception and minority experience can have explosive consequences. Little more than a year after the 1992 Los Angeles rebellion, a sixteen-year-old high school junior shared her opinions with a reporter from the *Los Angeles Times*. "I don't think white people owe anything to black people," she explained. "We didn't sell them into slavery, it was our ancestors. What they did was wrong, but we've done our best to make up for it." A seventeen-year-old senior echoed those comments, telling the reporter, "I feel we spend more time in my history class talking about what whites owe blacks than just about anything else when the issue of slavery comes up. I often received dirty looks. This seems strange given that I wasn't even alive then. And the few members of my family from that time didn't have the luxury of owning much, let alone slaves. So why, I ask you, am I constantly made to feel guilty?"[69]

More ominously, after pleading guilty to bombing two homes and one car, vandalizing a synagogue, and attempting to start a race war by planning the murder of Rodney King and the bombing of Los Angeles's First African Methodist Episcopal Church, twenty-year-old Christopher David Fisher explained that "sometimes whites were picked on because of the color of their skin. . . . Maybe we're blamed for slavery."[70] Fisher's actions were certainly extreme, but his justification of them drew knowingly and precisely on a broadly shared narrative about the victimization of "innocent" whites by irrational and ungrateful minorities.

The comments and questions raised about the legacy of slavery by these young whites illuminate broader currents in our culture, with enormous implications for understanding the enduring significance of race in our country. These young people associate black grievances solely with slavery, and they express irritation at what they perceive as efforts to make them feel guilty or unduly privileged because of things that happened in the distant past. The claim that one's own family did not own any slaves is frequently voiced in our culture. It is almost never followed with a statement to the effect that of course some people's families did own slaves and we will not rest until we track them down and make them pay reparations. This view never acknowledges how the existence of slavery and the exploitation of black labor after emancipation created opportunities from which immigrants and others benefited, even if they did not personally own slaves. Rather, it seems to hold that, because not all white people owned slaves, no white people can be held accountable or inconvenienced by the legacy of slavery. More important, having dispensed with slavery, they feel no need to address the histories of Jim Crow segregation, racialized social policies, urban renewal, or the revived racism of contemporary neoconservatism. On the contrary, Fisher felt that his discomfort with being "picked on" and "blamed" for slavery gave him good reason to bomb homes, deface synagogues, and plot to kill black people.

Unfortunately for our society, these young whites accurately reflect the logic of the language of liberal individualism and its ideological predispositions in discussions of race. In their apparent ignorance of the disciplined, systemic, and collective *group* activity that has structured white identities in U.S. history, they are in good company. In a 1979 law journal article, future Supreme Court Justice Antonin Scalia argued that affirmative action "is based upon concepts of racial indebtedness and racial entitlement rather than individual worth and individual need" and is thus "racist."[71] Yet liberal individualism is not completely color-blind on this issue. As Cheryl I. Harris demonstrates, the legacy of liberal individualism has not prevented the Supreme Court from recognizing and protecting the group interests of *whites* in the Bakke, Croson, and Wygant cases.[72] In each case, the Court nullified affirmative action programs because they judged efforts to help blacks as harmful to whites: to white expectations of entitlement, expectations based on the possessive investment in whiteness they held as members of a group. In the Bakke case, for instance, where the plaintiff argued that medical school affirmative action programs disadvantaged white applicants like himself, neither Bakke nor the Court contested the legitimacy of medical school admissions standards that reserved five seats in each class for children of wealthy donors to the university or that penalized Bakke for being older than most of the other applicants. The group rights of not-wealthy people or of people older than their classmates did not compel the Court or Bakke to make any claim of harm. But they did challenge and reject a policy designed to offset the effects of past and present discrimination when they could construe the medical school admission policies as detrimental to the interests of whites as a group—and as a consequence they applied the "strict scrutiny" standard to protect whites while denying that protection to people of color. In this case, as in so many others, the language of liberal individualism serves as a cover for coordinated collective group interests.

Group interests are not monolithic, and aggregate figures can obscure serious differences within racial groups. All whites do not benefit from the possessive investment in whiteness in precisely the same ways; the experiences of members of minority groups are not interchangeable. But the possessive investment in whiteness always affects individual and group life chances and opportunities. Even in cases where minority groups secure political and economic power through collective mobilization, the terms and conditions of their collectivity and the logic of group solidarity are always influenced and intensified by the absolute value of whiteness in U.S. politics, economics, and culture.[73]

In the 1960s, members of the Black Panther Party used to say that "if you're not part of the solution, you're part of the problem." But those of us who are "white" can only become part of the solution if we recognize the degree to which we are already part of the problem—not because of our race, but because of our possessive investment in it. Neither conservative "free market" policies nor liberal social welfare policies can solve the "white problem" in the United States, because both reinforce the possessive investment in whiteness. . . .

Failure to acknowledge our society's possessive investment in whiteness prevents us from facing the present openly and honestly. It hides from us the devastating costs of disinvestment in America's infrastructure over the past two decades and keeps us from facing our responsibility to reinvest in human resources by channeling resources toward education, health, and housing—and away from subsidies for speculation and luxury. After two decades of disinvestment, the only further disinvestment we need is from the ruinous pathology of whiteness, which has always undermined our own best instincts and interests.

NOTES

The epigraph is from Baldwin, *The Devil Finds Work*, 1.

1. Raphael Tardon, "Richard Wright Tells Us: The White Problem in the United States," *Action*, October 24, 1946. Reprinted in Kenneth Kinnamon and Michel Fabre, *Conversations with Richard Wright* (Jackson: University Press of Mississippi, 1993), 99. Malcolm X and others used this same formulation in the 1960s, but I believe that it originated with Wright, or at least that is the earliest citation I have found.

2. Toni Morrison points out the ways in which African Americans play an essential role in the white imagination, how their representations both hide and reveal the terms of white supremacy upon which the nation was founded and has been sustained ever since. See *Playing in the Dark: Whiteness in the Literary Imagination* (Cambridge: Harvard University Press, 1992).

3. Richard Dyer, "White," *Screen* 29, 4 (fall 1998): 44.

4. I thank Michael Schudson for pointing out to me that since the passage of civil rights legislation in the 1960s whiteness dares not speak its name, cannot speak in its own behalf, but rather advances through a color-blind language radically at odds with the distinctly racialized distribution of resources and life chances in U.S. society.

5. Walter Benjamin, "Madame Ariane: Second Courtyard on the Left," in *One-Way Street* (London: New Left Books, 1969), 98–99.

6. See Lisa Lowe, *Immigrant Acts: On Asian American Cultural Politics* (Durham, N.C.: Duke University Press, 1996), 11–16; Gary B. Nash, *Red, White, and Black: The Peoples of Early America* (Englewood Cliffs, N.J.: Prentice-Hall, 1974); Ronald Takaki, *A Different Mirror: A History of Multicultural America* (Boston: Little, Brown, 1993), 177–83.

7. Nash, *Red, White, and Black*, 292–93.

8. See Kenneth Jackson, *Crabgrass Frontier: The Suburbanization of the United States* (New York: Oxford University Press, 1985), and Douglas S. Massey and Nancy A. Denton, *American Apartheid: Segregation and the Making of the Underclass* (Cambridge: Harvard University Press, 1993).

9. I thank Phil Ethington for pointing out to me that these aspects of New Deal policies emerged out of political negotiations between the segregationist Dixiecrats and liberals from the North and West. My perspective is that white supremacy was not a gnawing aberration within the New Deal coalition but rather an essential point of unity between southern whites and northern white ethnics.

10. Records of the Federal Home Loan Bank Board of the Home Owners Loan Corporation, City Survey File, Los Angeles, 1939, Neighborhood D-53, National Archives, Box 74, RG 195.

11. Massey and Denton, *American Apartheid*, 54.

12. John R. Logan and Harvey Molotch, *Urban Fortunes: The Political Economy of Place* (Berkeley and Los Angeles: University of California Press, 1987), 182.

13. Ibid., 114.

14. Arlene Zarembka, *The Urban Housing Crisis: Social, Economic, and Legal Issues and Proposals* (Westport, Conn.: Greenwood, 1990), 104.

15. Jill Quadagno, *The Color of Welfare: How Racism Undermined the War on Poverty* (New York: Oxford University Press, 1994), 92, 91.

16. Logan and Molotch, *Urban Fortunes*, 130.

17. See Gary Gerstle, "Working-Class Racism: Broaden the Focus," *International Labor and Working Class History* 44 (fall 1993): 36.

18. Logan and Molotch, *Urban Fortunes*, 168–69.

19. Troy Duster, "Crime, Youth Unemployment, and the Underclass," *Crime and Delinquency* 33, 2 (April 1987): 308, 309.

20. Massey and Denton, *American Apartheid*, 55.

21. Quadagno, *The Color of Welfare*, 105, 113; Massey and Denton, *American Apartheid*, 204–5.

22. Logan and Molotch, *Urban Fortunes*, 113.

23. Robert D. Bullard, "Environmental Justice for All," in *Unequal Protection: Environmental Justice and Communities of Color*, ed. Robert Bullard (San Francisco: Sierra Club, 1994), 9–10.

24. Robert D. Bullard, "Anatomy of Environmental Racism and the Environmental Justice Movement," in *Confronting Environmental Racism: Voices from the Grass Roots,* ed. Robert D. Bullard (Boston: South End, 1993), 21.

25. Bullard, "Environmental Justice for All," 13.

26. Charles Lee, "Beyond Toxic Wastes and Race," in *Confronting Environmental Racism: Voices from the Grass Roots,* ed. Robert D. Bullard (Boston: South End, 1993), 49. Two corporate-sponsored research institutes challenged claims of racial bias in the location and operation of toxic and hazardous waste systems. Andy B. Anderson, Douglas L. Anderton, and John Michael Oakes made the corporate case in "Environmental Equity: Evaluating TSDF Siting over the Past Two Decades," *Waste Age,* July 1994. These results were trumpeted in a report by the Washington University Center for the Study of American Business, funded by the John M. Olin Foundation. But the study by Anderson, Anderton, and Oakes was sponsored by the Institute of Chemical Waste Management, an industry trade group. The researchers claimed that their results were not influenced by corporate sponsorship, but they limited their inquiry to urban areas with toxic storage, disposal, and treatment facilities, conveniently excluding seventy facilities, 15 percent of TSDFs, and 20 percent of the population. The world's largest waste company, WMX Company, contributed $250,000 to the study, and the study's research plan excluded from scrutiny two landfills owned by WMX: the nation's largest commercial landfill, located in the predominately African American city of Emelle, Alabama, and the nation's fifth largest landfill, in Kettelman City Hills, California, a predominately Latino community.

27. Bunyan Bryant and Paul Mohai, *Race and the Incidence of Environmental Hazards* (Boulder, Colo.: Westview, 1992).

28. Lee, "Beyond Toxic Wastes and Race," 48.

29. Robert D. Bullard, "Decision Making," in Laura Westra and Peter S. Wenz, eds., *Faces of Environmental Racism: Confronting Issues of Global Justice* (Lanham, MD: Rowman and Littlefield, 1995), 4.

30. Bullard, "Anatomy of Environmental Racism," 21.

31. David L.L. Shields, "What Color Is Hunger?" in David L.L. Shields, ed., *The Color of Hunger: Race and Hunger in National and International Perspective* (Lanham, MD: Rowman and Littlefield, 1996), 4.

32. Centers for Disease Control, "Nutritional Status of Minority Children: United States, 1986," *Morbidity and Mortality Weekly Reports (MMWR)* 36, 23 (June, 19, 1987): 366–69.

33. Peter S. Wenz, "Just Garbage," in Laura Westra and Peter S. Wenz, eds., *Faces of Environmental Racism: Confronting Issues of Global Justice* (Lanham, MD: Rowman and Littlefield, 1996), 66; Robert D. Bullard, "Decision Making," in Laura Westra and Peter S., Wenz, eds., *Faces of Environmental Racism,* 8.

34. Laura Pulido, "Multiracial Organizing Among Environmental Justice Activists in Los Angeles," in Michael J. Dear, H. Eric Shockman, and Greg Hise, eds., *Rethinking Los Angeles* (Thousand Oaks, CA, London, New Delhi: Sage, 1996): 175.

35. Charles Trueheart, "The Bias Most Deadly," *Washington Post,* October 30, 1990, sec. 7, cited in Shields, *The Color of Hunger,* 3.

36. George Anders, "Disparities in Medicare Access Found Among Poor, Black or Disabled Patients," *Wall Street Journal,* November 2, 1994; Lina R. Godfrey, "Institutional Discrimination and Satisfaction with Specific Government Services by Heads of Households in Ten Southern States," paper presented at the Rural Sociological Society annual meeting, 1984, cited in Shields, *The Color of Hunger,* 6, 13.

37. Jeffrey Shotland, *Full Fields, Empty Cupboards: The Nutritional Status of Migrant Farm-workers in America* (Washington: Public Voice for Food and Health: 1989) cited in Shields, *The Color of Hunger,* 3.

38. Linda A. Wray, "Health Policy and Ethnic Diversity in Older Americans: Dissonance or Harmony," *Western Journal of Medicine* 157, 3 (September 1992): 357–61.

39. Eva Bertram, Morris Blachman, Kenneth Sharpe, and Peter Andreas, *Drug War Politics: The Price of Denial* (Berkeley and Los Angeles: University of California Press, 1996), 38–42; Alexander C. Lichtenstein and Michael A. Kroll, "The Fortress Economy: The Economic Role of the U.S. Prison System," in Elihu Rosenblatt, ed., *Criminal Injustice: Confronting the Prison Crisis* (Boston: South End, 1996), 21, 25–26.

40. Ibid., 41.

41. Massey and Denton, *American Apartheid,* 61.

42. Gertrude Ezorsky, *Racism and Justice: The Case for Affirmative Action* (Ithaca, N.Y.: Cornell University Press, 1991), 25.

43. Logan and Molotch, *Urban Fortunes,* 116.

44. Jim Campen, "Lending Insights: Hard Proof That Banks Discriminate," *Dollars and Sense,* January–February 1991, 17.

45. Mitchell Zuckoff, "Study Shows Racial Bias in Lending," *Boston Globe,* October 9, 1992.

46. Paul Ong and J. Eugene Grigsby III, "Race and Life-Cycle Effects on Home Ownership in Los Angeles, 1970 to 1980," *Urban Affairs Quarterly* 23, 4 (June 1988): 605.

47. Massey and Denton, *American Apartheid,* 108.

48. Gary Orfield and Carol Ashkinaze, *The Closing Door: Conservative Policy and Black Opportunity* (Chicago: University of Chicago Press, 1991), 58, 78.

49. Logan and Molotch, *Urban Fortunes,* 129.

50. Campen, "Lending Insights," 18.

51. Alicia H. Munnell, Lyn E. Browne, James McEneany, and Geoffrey M. B. Tootel, "Mortgage Lending in Boston: Interpreting HMDA Data" (Boston: Federal Reserve Bank of Boston, 1993); Kimberly Blanton, "Fed Blocks Shawmut's Bid to Gain N.H. Bank," *Boston Globe,* November 16, 1993.

52. Ellis Cose, *Rage of a Privileged Class* (New York: HarperCollins, 1993), 191.

53. Gregory Squires, "'Runaway Plants,' Capital Mobility, and Black Economic Rights," in *Community and Capital in Conflict: Plant Closings and Job Loss,* ed. John C. Raines, Lenora E. Berson, and David McI. Gracie (Philadelphia: Temple University Press, 1983), 70.

54. Ezorsky, *Racism and Justice,* 15.

55. Orfield and Ashkinaze, *The Closing Door,* 225–26.

56. Peter Downs, "Tax Abatements Don't Work," *St. Louis Journalism Review,* February 1997, 16.

57. "State Taxes Gouge the Poor, Study Says," *Long Beach Press-Telegram,* April 23, 1991, sec. A.

58. "Proposition 13," *UC Focus,* June/July 1993, 2.

59. William Chafe, *The Unfinished Journey* (New York: Oxford University Press, 1986), 442; Noel J. Kent, "A Stacked Deck: Racial Minorities and the New American Political Economy," *Explorations in Ethnic Studies* 14, 1 (January 1991): 11.

60. Carey Goldberg, "Hispanic Households Struggle as Poorest of the Poor in the U.S.," *New York Times,* January 30, 1997, sec. A.

61. Kent, "A Stacked Deck," 13.

62. Melvin Oliver and James Johnson, "Economic Restructuring and Black Male Joblessness in United States Metropolitan Areas," *Urban Geography* 12, 6 (November–December 1991); Gerald David Jaynes and Robin M. Williams, Jr., eds., *A Common Destiny: Blacks and American Society* (Washington, D.C.: National Academy Press, 1989); Reynolds Farley and Walter R. Allen, *The Color Line and the Quality of Life in America* (New York: Russell Sage Foundation, 1987); Melvin Oliver and Tom Shapiro, "Wealth of a Nation: A Reassessment of Asset Inequality in America Shows at Least One-Third of Households Are Asset Poor," *Journal of Economics and Sociology* 49, 2 (April 1990); Jonathan Kozol, *Savage Inequalities: Children in America's Schools* (New York: Crown, 1991); Cornell West, *Race Matters* (Boston: Beacon, 1993).

63. Orfield and Ashkinaze, *The Closing Door,* 46, 206.

64. Bart Landry, "The Enduring Dilemma of Race in America," in *America at Century's End,* ed. Alan H. Wolfe (Berkeley and Los Angeles: University of California Press, 1991), 206; John Hope Franklin, *The Color Line: Legacy for the Twenty-First Century* (Columbia: University of Missouri Press, 1993), 36–37.

65. Kathleen Hall Jamieson, *Dirty Politics: Deception, Distraction, and Democracy* (New York: Oxford University Press, 1992), 100.

66. Thomas Byrne Edsall and Mary D. Edsall, *Chain Reaction: The Impact of Race, Rights, and Taxes on American Politics* (New York: Norton, 1991).

67. Nathan Glazer makes this argument in *Affirmative Discrimination* (New York: Basic Books, 1975).

68. I borrow the term "overdetermination" from Louis Althusser, who uses it to show how dominant ideologies become credible to people in part because various institutions and agencies independently replicate them and reinforce their social power.

69. Rogena Schuyler, "Youth: We Didn't Sell Them into Slavery," *Los Angeles Times,* June 21, 1993, sec. B.

70. Jim Newton, "Skinhead Leader Pleads Guilty to Violence, Plot," *Los Angeles Times,* October 20, 1993, sec. A.

71. Antonin Scalia, "The Disease as Cure," *Washington University Law Quarterly,* no. 147 (1979): 153–54, quoted in Cheryl I. Harris, "Whiteness as Property," *Harvard Law Review* 106, 8 (June 1993): 1767.

72. Harris, ibid., 1993.

73. The rise of a black middle class and the setbacks suffered by white workers during deindustrialization may seem to subvert the analysis presented here. Yet the black middle class remains fragile, far less able than other middle-class groups to translate advances in income into advances in wealth and power. Similarly, the success of neoconservatism since the 1970s has rested on securing support from white workers for economic policies that do them objective harm by mobilizing counter-subversive electoral coalitions against busing and affirmative action, while carrying out attacks on public institutions and resources by representing "public" space as black space. See Oliver and Shapiro, "Wealth of a Nation." See also Logan and Molotch, *Urban Fortunes*.

Global White Supremacy

Charles W. Mills

"White supremacy is the unnamed political system that has made the modern world what it is today." That was the opening sentence of a book I published ten years ago, *The Racial Contract.*[1] In the following short summary, drawing on sections of the book, I am going to try to explain and defend this claim. Perhaps after reading my summary, some readers will be interested enough that they will seek out the original.

I

How could white supremacy possibly be, or have been, *global,* a system that has "made the modern world what it is today"? Even if people concede (as many are still reluctant to do) that the United States was once a white-supremacist state, they would quickly point out that that doesn't say anything about the rest of the world.

The problem here is a combination of historical amnesia (a forgetting of the facts) and conceptual blindness (a failure to admit the implications of those facts, even when remembered). We need to see the European expansion over the world in the modern period for what it is—not as voyages of "discovery" but as missions of *conquest*, a conquest that, in the words of V. G. Kiernan, made them "the lords of human kind."[2] In effect, Europeans came to rule the world.

Consider the history. The United States itself, of course, is a white settler state established on territory expropriated from its aboriginal inhabitants through a combination of military force, disease, and hundreds of broken treaties. George Washington, Father of the Nation, was, understandably, known somewhat differently to the Senecas as "Town Destroyer." In the Declaration of Independence, Thomas Jefferson characterized Native Americans as "merciless Indian Savages," while his inspiring opening sentence—"We hold these truths to be self-evident: that all men are created equal"—was evidently not meant to apply to the black slaves he owned. So the American polity was created as a racial one, in which only whites got to be full persons and equal citizens, with nonwhites being sub-persons and non- or at best second-class citizens.

But the point is that the United States is not unique. Though on a smaller scale and not always so ruthlessly . . . the other white settler states—for example, Canada, Australia, New Zealand, South Africa—were all founded on similar policies: the extermination, displacement, and/or herding onto reservations of the aboriginal population. And until a few decades ago, all imposed racially restrictive immigration rules, aimed at maintaining a "white" nation.

Elsewhere, in Latin America, Asia, and Africa, large parts of the world were colonized, that is, formally brought under the rule of one or another of the European powers (or, later, the United States): the early Spanish and Portuguese empires in the Americas, the Philippines, and south Asia; the jealous competition from Britain, France, and Holland; the British conquest of India; the French expansion into Algeria and Indochina; the Dutch advance into Indonesia; the Opium Wars against China; the late nineteenth-century "scramble for Africa"; the U.S. war against Spain, seizure of Cuba, Puerto Rico, and the Philippines, and annexation of Hawaii.

So in those colonized nations which only became independent after World War II, whites ruled formally, and in countries which became independent at a relatively early stage, in the eighteenth, nineteenth, and beginning of the twentieth centuries, like the United States, the Latin American nations, Australia, and others, whites were politically dominant, with people of color (Native Americans and Australians; black, Mexican, and Asian North Americans; black, *indio*, mulatto, and *mestizo* Latin Americans) being formally or informally subordinated. In fact, if we were to go back in a time machine a hundred years, to the early twentieth century, we would find a world more than 90% of which was controlled by whites. The few exceptions—such as Japan, which was never colonized, or Haiti, famous for having the only successful slave revolution in history—still had to operate in a white-ruled world.

Moreover, this racial dichotomization was not incidental. It was not just that the rulers happened to be white and the subjected happened to be nonwhite. Rather, race was absolutely central to the justificatory ideology of the period. It was precisely *because* of alleged white superiority to other races that whites saw themselves as entitled to rule over them. In fact, the phrase originally used for nonwhites—a phrase that is today an embarrassment for whites—was "subject races," making their inequality clear. The long history of derogatory terms for people of color—niggers, injuns, chinks, wogs, darkies, greasers, blackfellows, kaffirs, coolies, abos, dinks, googoos, gooks—is not a matter of idiosyncratic individual white racism. Rather, it reflects the reality of a world that was objectively divided between the racially dominant and the racially subordinated, between "men" and "natives," the "civilized" and the "savage." A two-tiered moral and legal code was created, based on the principle that one set of rules obtained for whites (persons) and another for nonwhites (sub-persons).

The "Doctrine of Discovery," for example, stated that as "infidels, heathens, and savages," Native Americans had no "right of property and dominion" over their land, which was "deemed as if it were inhabited only by brute animals," so that Europeans gained "an absolute dominion" over these territories "as a right acquired by discovery." In the 1857 *Dred Scott* v. *Sanford* U.S. Supreme Court decision, Chief Justice Roger Taney wrote that blacks "had no rights which the white man was bound to respect; and that the Negro might justly and lawfully be reduced to slavery for his benefit." A French colonial theorist, Jules Harmand, explained matter-of-factly that "It is necessary, then, to accept as a principle and point of departure the fact that there is a hierarchy of races and civilizations, and that we belong to the superior race and civilization. . . . Our dignity rests on that quality, and it underlies our right to direct the rest of humanity."

So racism was not an anomaly, a deviation from the norm. Racism *was* the norm. In effect, European humanism usually meant that only Europeans were human. One could say that European expansionism created a transnational white polity, a virtual community of people linked by their citizenship in Europe at home and abroad . . . and constituted in opposition to their indigenous subjects. In most of Africa and Asia, where colonial rule ended only after World War II, rigid "color bars" maintained the separation between Europeans and natives. As European, as white, one knew oneself to be a member of the superior race, one's skin being one's passport. So though there were local variations in the patterns of racial domination—for example, a bipolar racial system in the (Anglo) United States, as against a subtler color hierarchy in (Iberian) Latin America—it remained the case that the white tribe, as the global representative of civilization and modernity, was generally on top of the social pyramid.

The modern world was thus expressly created as a racially hierarchical polity, globally dominated by Europeans. In the Treaty of Tordesillas (1494) which divided the planet between Spain and Portugal, the Valladolid, Spain, Conference (1550–51) to decide whether Native Americans were really human, the later debates over African slavery and abolitionism, the Berlin Conference (1884–85) to partition Africa, the various intra-European pacts, treaties, and informal arrangements on policing their colonies, the 1919 post–World War I Versailles Conference in which the Japanese delegation's proposal to include "the equality of races" in the League of Nations' Covenant was formally defeated,

we see (or should see) with complete clarity a world being governed by
white people. . . .

II

Against this background, we can now appreciate why the moral and political theory, and the practical struggles of nonwhites, have so often centered on *race.* Everywhere in the Native American, black American, and
Third and Fourth World anti-colonial thought one can find a recognition
of the person/sub-person differentiation, the correspondingly racially
structured moral code, and the white-supremacist character of the polity.

Sitting Bull asks: "What treaty that the whites have kept has the red man
broken? Not one. What treaty that the white man ever made with us have
they kept? Not one. When I was a boy the Sioux owned the world; the sun
rose and set on their land. . . . Where are our lands? Who owns them?"
Marcus Garvey concludes that blacks are "a race without respect." Jawaharlal Nehru claims that British policy in India is "that of the herrenvolk and
the master race." Malcolm X asserts that: "We are fighting for recognition
as human beings." Frantz Fanon maps a colonial world divided between
"two different species," a "governing race" and "zoological" natives. Australian Aborigines in a 1982 protest statement point out that "since the
White invasion . . . our humanity is being degraded and our history dis-
torted by strangers. . . . *We hereby demand yet again recognition of our humanity
and our land rights.*" The central moral commonality uniting all their experiences is the reality of racial subordination, necessarily generating a different moral topography from the one standardly examined in white
ethnical discourse.

Correspondingly, the polity was usually thought of in racial terms, as
white-ruled, and this perspective would become global in the period of
formal colonial administration. Political theory is in part about who the
main actors are, and for this unacknowledged polity they are neither the
atomic individuals of classic liberal thought nor the classes of Marxist theory but races. The various native and colonial peoples' attempts . . . to
forge a *racial* unity—Pan-Indianism, Pan-Africanism, Pan-Arabism, Pan-
Asianism, Pan-Islamism—arose in response to an *already achieved* white
unity, a Pan-Europeanism.

In the period of de jure global white supremacy, of colonialism and slavery, this solidarity was clearly perceived by whites also. "That race is everything, is simply a fact," wrote Scotsman Robert Knox in *The Races of Men*
(1850), and theories of the necessity of racial struggle, race war, against the
subordinate races were put forward as obvious. Darwin's work raised hopes
in some quarters that natural selection (perhaps with a little help from its
friends) would sweep away the remaining inferior races, as it had already
done so providentially in the Americas and Tasmania, so that the planet as a
whole could be cleared for white settlement. And after that only the sky

would be the limit. In fact, even the sky would *not* be the limit, for there was always the solar system. Cecil Rhodes dreamed that perhaps he could "annex the planets" for Britain: "Where there is space, there is hope."

But alas, this noble dream was not to be realized. Even with encouragement, nonwhites did not die fast enough. So whites had to settle for colonial rule over stubbornly growing native populations, while of course keeping a watchful eye out for both rebellion and subversive notions of self-government. Witness the various colored perils—Red (Native American, that is), black, and yellow—that have haunted the European and Euro-implanted imagination. "Europe," V. G. Kiernan comments, "thought of its identity in terms of race or color and plagued itself with fears of the Yellow Peril or a Black Peril—boomerang effects, as they might be called, of a White Peril from which the other continents were more tangibly suffering."[3] The political framework was quite explicitly predicated on the notion that whites everywhere had a common interest in maintaining global white supremacy against insurrections conceived of in racial terms. At the turn of the twentieth century, Europeans were worried about the "vast ant-heap" filled with "soldier-ants" of China, while "similar fears were in the air about a huge black army," threatening a race war of revenge led by "dusky Napoleons."[4]

Though there were occasional breaches for strategic national advantage, international white racial solidarity was generally demonstrated in the joint actions to suppress and isolate slave rebellions and colonial uprisings: the boycott of Haiti, the only successful slave revolution in history (and, noncoincidentally, today the poorest country in the Western Hemisphere), the common intervention against the 1899–1900 Boxer rebellion in China, the concern raised by the 1905 Japanese victory over Russia. As late as the early twentieth century, books were still being published with such warning titles as *The Passing of the Great Race* (Madison Grant, 1916) and *The Rising Tide of Color against White World-Supremacy* (Lothrop Stoddard, 1920). Intra-European differences and conflicts were real enough but would be quickly put aside in the face of the nonwhite threat: "When it came to any serious colonial upheaval, white men felt their kinship, and Europe drew together. . . . Above all, and very remarkably, despite innumerable crises over rival claims the European countries managed from the War of American Independence onward to avoid a single colonial war among themselves."[5]

This unity ended in the twentieth century with the outbreak of World War I, which was in part an inter-imperialist war over competing colonial claims. But despite nonwhite political agitation and military participation in the armies of their respective mother countries, the postwar settlement led not to decolonization but to a territorial redistribution among the colonial powers themselves. ("OK, I'll take this one, and you can take that one.") In the interwar years Japan's Pan-Asiatic Greater East Asia Co-Prosperity Sphere was seen by most white Western leaders as a threat to global white supremacy. Indeed, as late as World War II, the popular American writer Pearl Buck had to warn her readers that colonized peoples would not continue to put up with global white domination, and that unless there was change their discontent would lead to "the longest of human wars . . . the war between the white man and his world and the colored man and his world."

Corresponding to this global white solidarity transcending national boundaries, the virtual white polity, nonwhites' common oppression manifested itself in patterns of partisan emotional identification that from a modern, more nationalistic perspective now seem quite bizarre. In 1879, for example, when the King of Burma learned of the Zulu defeat of a British army at Isandhlwana, he immediately announced his intention of marching on Rangoon. In 1905 Indians cheered the Japanese victory over the czar's (white) armies in the Russo-Japanese War. In the Spanish-American War, black Americans raised doubts about the point of being "a black man in the army of the white man sent to kill the brown man," and a few blacks actually went over to the side of Emilio Aguinaldo's Filipino forces. After Pearl Harbor, the ominous joke circulated in the American press of a black sharecropper who comments to his white boss, "By the way, Cap'n, I hear the Japs done declared war on you white folks"; black civil rights militants demanded the "double-V," "Victory at Home as Well as Abroad"; Japanese intelligence considered the possibility of an alliance with black Americans in a domestic colored front against white supremacy; and white Americans worried about black loyalty. The 1954 Vietnamese victory over the French at Dien Bien Phu (like the Japanese capture of Singapore in World War II) was in part seen as a *racial* triumph, the defeat of a white by a brown people, a blow against the arrogance of global white supremacy.

So on the level of the popular consciousness of nonwhites, racial self-identification was deeply embedded. The different battles around the world against slavery, colonialism, Jim Crow, the "color bar," European imperialism, apartheid, were in a sense all part of a common struggle against global white supremacy, so that a victory for one was a victory for all. . . .

Today, correspondingly, though formal decolonization has taken place and in Africa and Asia black, brown, and yellow natives are in office, ruling independent nations, the global economy is essentially dominated by the former colonial powers, their offshoots (Euro–United States, Euro-Canada), and their international financial institutions, lending agencies, and corporations. (The notable exception, whose history confirms rather than challenges the rule, is Japan, which escaped colonization and, after the Meiji Restoration, successfully embarked on its own industrialization.) Global figures on income and property ownership are, of course, broken down nationally rather than racially, but if a transnational racial disaggregation were to be done, it would reveal that whites control a percentage of the world's wealth grossly disproportionate to their numbers. This globally color-coded distribution of wealth and poverty has been produced by the legacy of global white supremacy. But the connection between the development of the European and Euro-implanted nation-state's industry, culture, and civilization, and the material and cultural contributions of Afro-Asia and the Americas is denied, so that Europeans and their descendants seem peculiarly rational and industrious, differentially endowed with qualities that have enabled them to dominate the world. Other parts of the world then disappear from the white political history, subsumed under the general category of risible non-European space, the "Third World," where for reasons of local folly and geographical blight the inspiring model of the self-sufficient white polity cannot be followed. The ever-deepening abyss between the First World and the Third World, where millions—largely nonwhite—die of starvation each year and many more hundreds of millions—also largely nonwhite—live in wretched poverty, is seen as unfortunate (calling, certainly, for the occasional charitable contribution), but unrelated to the history of transcontinental and intracontinental racial exploitation.

Moreover, it is not merely that Europe and the former white settler states are globally dominant but that *within* them, where there is a significant nonwhite presence (indigenous peoples, descendants of imported slaves, voluntary nonwhite immigration), whites continue to be advantaged vis-à-vis nonwhites. So if in the period of de jure white supremacy, white domination was explicit, in the present period it has been written out of formal existence. Racial discriminatory practices continue, of course, if not on the same scale as before. But even apart from these, a crucial manifestation of ongoing white privilege is simply *the failure to ask certain questions*, the taking for granted as a status quo and baseline the existing racialized configurations of wealth, poverty, property, and opportunities, the pretence that formal, juridical equality is sufficient to remedy inequities created on a foundation of several hundred years of racial privilege. That as recently as 2001, the median net worth of white American households was fourteen times the median net worth of black American households is not seen as connected to the history of black subordination, but as a reflection of black unwillingness to work.

III

If to white readers this history, less than a century distant, now seems like an alien universe, it is a tribute to the success of a self-transforming white supremacy in rewriting the terms of public discourse so that white domination is now conceptually invisible. But the history is real. The struggle to close the gap between the modern ideal of the liberal democratic policy and the modern reality of the white-supremacist polity has been the unacknowledged political history of the past few hundred years, the "battle of the color line," in the words of W. E. B. Du Bois. Moreover, it is likely to continue being so for the near future, as racial division continues to fester, the United States moves demographically from a white-majority to a nonwhite-majority society, the chasm between a largely white First World and a largely nonwhite Third World continues to deepen, desperate illegal immigration from the latter to the former escalates, and demands for global justice grow louder. Naming this reality—global white supremacy— is a crucial prerequisite for these issues to be honestly addressed. Until whites can admit this history, they will continue to be complicit with it.

NOTES

1. Charles W. Mills, *The Racial Contract* (Ithaca, NY: Cornell University Press, 1997), p. 1.

2. V. G. Kiernan, *The Lords of Human Kind: Black Man, Yellow Man, and White Man in an Age of Empire* (1969; reprint, New York: Columbia University Press, 1986).

3. V. G. Kiernan, *Imperialism and Its Contradictions*, ed. Harvey J. Kaye (New York: Routledge, 1995), p. 146.

4. Kiernan, *Lords*, pp. 171, 237.

5. Kiernan, *Lords*, p. 27.

QUESTIONS FOR THINKING, WRITING, AND DISCUSSION FOR PART TWO

1. According to Wander, Martin, and Nakayama, what role did science play in helping to justify conquest and slavery during the colonial period? Do you think a case can be made for the claim that science continues to play such a role today? If so, how; if not, why not?

2. The third selection in Part Two is titled "How White People Became White." At least on first reading, this title appears puzzling. Explain the title.

3. How does Karen Brodkin support her claim that educational and occupational GI benefits provided after World War II really constituted an affirmative action program for white males? Would George Lipsitz, whose article also appears in Part Two, agree or disagree with this claim? How about you? Do you agree or disagree—and why?

4. Drawing on the essays by Brodkin and Lipsitz, construct the most powerful argument you can in support of the claim that white privilege has been institutionalized and protected by U.S. government policy over the years; then go on to agree or disagree with the argument you have made.

5. Does Neil Foley equate becoming Hispanic with becoming white? According to his essay, are all Mexican Americans currently considered white in the United States? Compare and contrast Foley's account of how some Mexican Americans came to be categorized as white with the accounts of how members of other ethnic groups (for example, Greeks and Poles) came to be included in this category.

6. How are Asian Americans viewed in the United States? How is their relationship to whiteness similar to or different from the situation of Mexican Americans as described in the Foley article?

7. Charles W. Mills makes a strong case for his view that white supremacy has been the unacknowledged operating political system in the world throughout recorded time. Evaluate this claim and indicate what you believe to be the strongest arguments in its favor.

8. If you learned some new information by reading Mills's piece, do some independent research to corroborate what you have learned and write an essay in which you lay out these new facts and speculate about why you were not taught or did not know them previously.

9. What does it mean to claim that whiteness has been socially constructed?

part

3 three

**whiteness:
the power of
privilege**

Making Systems of Privilege Visible

—Stephanie M. Wildman with Adrienne D. Davis

The notion of privilege, although part of the consciousness of popular culture, has not been recognized in legal language and doctrine. This failure to acknowledge privilege, to make it visible in legal doctrine, creates a serious gap in legal reasoning, rendering us unable to address issues of systemic unfairness.

The invisibility of privilege strengthens the power it creates and maintains. The invisible cannot be combated, and as a result privilege is allowed to perpetuate, regenerate, and re-create itself. Privilege is systemic, not an occasional occurrence. Privilege is invisible only until looked for, but silence in the face of privilege sustains its invisibility.

Silence is the lack of sound and voice. Silence may result from a desire for quiet; it may signify intense mental concentration; it may also arise from oppression or fear. Whatever the reason, when there is silence, no criticism is expressed. What we do not say, what we do not talk about, allows the status quo to continue. To describe these unspoken systems means we need to use language. But even when we try to talk about privilege, the language we use inhibits our ability to perceive the systems of privilege that constitute the status quo.

HOW LANGUAGE VEILS THE EXISTENCE OF SYSTEMS OF PRIVILEGE

Language contributes to the invisibility and regeneration of privilege. To begin the conversation about subordination, we sort ideas into categories such as race and gender. These words are part of a system of categorization that we use without thinking and that seems linguistically neutral. Race and gender are, after all, just words.

Yet when we learn that someone has had a child, our first question is usually "Is it a girl or a boy?" Why do we ask that, instead of something like "Are the mother and child healthy?" We ask, "Is it a girl or a boy?" according to philosopher Marilyn Frye, because we do not know how to relate to this new being without knowing its gender.[1] Imagine how long you could have a discussion with or about someone without knowing her or his gender. We place people into these categories because our world is gendered.

Similarly, our world is also raced, and it is hard for us to avoid taking mental notes as to race. We use our language to categorize by race, particularly, if we are white, when that race is other than white. Marge Shultz has written of calling on a Latino student in her class.[2] She called him Mr. Martínez, but his name was Rodríguez. The class tensed up at her error; earlier that same day another professor had called him Mr. Hernández, the name of the defendant in the criminal law case under discussion. Professor Shultz talked with her class, at its next session, about her error and how our thought processes lead us to categorize in order to think. She acknowledged how this process leads to stereotyping that causes pain to individuals. We all live in this raced and gendered world, inside these powerful categories, that make it hard to see each other as whole people.

But the problem does not stop with the general terms "race" and "gender." Each of these categories contains the images, like an entrance to a tunnel with many passages and arrows pointing down each possible path, of subcategories. Race is often defined as Black and white; sometimes it is defined as white and "of color." There are other races, and sometimes the categories are each listed, for example, as African American, Hispanic American, Asian American, Native American, and White American, if whiteness is mentioned at all. All these words, describing racial subcategories, seem neutral on their face, like equivalent titles. But however the subcategories are listed, however neutrally the words are expressed, these words mask a system of power, and that system privileges whiteness.

Gender, too, is a seemingly neutral category that leads us to imagine subcategories of male and female. A recent scientific article suggested that five genders might be a more accurate characterization of human anatomy, but there is a heavy systemic stake in our image of two genders.[3] The apparently neutral categories male and female mask the privileging of males that is part of the gender power system. Try to think of equivalent gendered titles, like king and queen, prince and princess, and you will quickly see that male and female are not equal titles in our cultural imagination.

Poet and social critic Adrienne Rich has written convincingly about the compulsory heterosexuality that is part of this gender power system.[4] Almost everywhere we look, heterosexuality is portrayed as the norm. In Olympic ice-skating and dancing, for example, a couple is defined as a man partnered with a woman.[5] Heterosexuality is privileged over any other relationship. The words we use, such as "marriage," "husband," and "wife," are not neutral, but convey this privileging of heterosexuality. What is amazing, says Rich, is that there are any lesbians or gay men at all.[6]

Our culture suppresses conversation about class privilege as well as race and gender privileges. Although we must have money or access to money to obtain human necessities such as food, clothing, and shelter, those fundamental needs are recognized only as an individual responsibility. The notion of privilege based on economic wealth is viewed as a radical, dangerous idea, or an idiosyncratic throwback to the past, conjuring up countries with monarchies, nobility, serfs, and peasants. Yet even the archaic vocabulary makes clear that no one wants to be categorized as a have-not. The economic power system is not invisible—everyone knows that money brings privilege. But the myth persists that all have access to that power through individual resourcefulness. This myth of potential economic equality supports the invisibility of the other power systems that prevent fulfillment of that ideal.

Other words we use to describe subordination also mask the operation of privilege. Increasingly, people use terms like "racism" and "sexism" to describe disparate treatment and the perpetuation of power. Yet this vocabulary of "isms" as a descriptive shorthand for undesirable, disadvantaging treatment creates several serious problems.

First, calling someone a racist individualizes the behavior and veils the fact that racism can occur only where it is culturally, socially, and legally supported. It lays the blame on the individual rather than the systemic forces that have shaped that individual and his or her society. White people know they do not want to be labeled racist; they become concerned with how to avoid that label, rather than worrying about systemic racism and how to change it.

Second, the isms language focuses on the larger category, such as race, gender, sexual preference. Isms language suggests that within these larger categories two seemingly neutral halves exist, equal parts in a mirror. Thus Black and white, male and female, heterosexual and gay/lesbian appear, through the linguistic juxtaposition, as equivalent subparts. In fact, although the category does not take note of it, Blacks and whites, men and women, heterosexuals and gays/lesbians are not equivalently situated in society. Thus the way we think and talk about the categories and subcategories that underlie the isms allows us to consider them parallel parts, and obscures the pattern of domination and subordination within each classification.

Similarly, the syllable "isms" itself gives the illusion that all patterns of domination and subordination are the same and interchangeable. The language suggests that someone subordinated under one form of oppression would be similarly situated to another person subordinated under another form. Thus, a person subordinated under one form may feel no need to view himself/herself as a possible oppressor, or beneficiary of oppression, within a different form. For example, white women, having an ism that defines their condition—sexism—may not look at the way they are privileged by racism. They have defined themselves as one of the oppressed.

Finally, the focus on individual behavior, the seemingly neutral subparts of categories, and the apparent interchangeability underlying the vocabulary of isms all obscure the existence of systems of privilege and power. It is difficult to see and talk about how oppression operates when the vocabulary itself makes these systems of privilege invisible. "White supremacy" is associated with a lunatic fringe, not with the everyday life of well-meaning white citizens. "Racism" is defined by whites in terms of specific, discriminatory racist actions by others. The vocabulary allows us to talk about discrimination and oppression, but it hides the mechanism that makes that oppression possible and efficient. It also hides the existence of specific, identifiable beneficiaries of oppression, who are not always the actual perpetrators of discrimination. The use of isms language, or any focus on discrimination, masks the privileging that is created by these systems of power.

Thus the very vocabulary we use to talk about discrimination obfuscates these power systems and the privilege that is their natural companion. To remedy discrimination effectively we must make the power systems and the privileges they create visible and part of the discourse. To move toward a unified theory of the dynamics of subordination, we have to find a way to talk about privilege. When we discuss race, sex, and sexual orientation, each needs to be described as a power system that creates privileges in some people as well as disadvantages in others. Most of the literature has focused on disadvantage or discrimination, ignoring the element of privilege. To really talk about these issues, privilege must be made visible.

WHAT IS PRIVILEGE?

What then is privilege? We all recognize its most blatant forms. "Men only admitted to this club." "We will not allow African Americans into that school." Blatant exercises of privilege certainly exist, but they are not what most people think of as our way of life. They are only the tip of the iceberg, however.

When we try to look at privilege we see several elements. First, the characteristics of the privileged group define the societal norm, often benefiting those in the privileged group. Second, privileged group members can rely on their privilege and avoid objecting to oppression. Both the conflation of privilege with the societal norm and the implicit option to ignore oppression mean that privilege is rarely seen by the holder of the privilege.

A. THE NORMALIZATION OF PRIVILEGE

The characteristics and attributes of those who are privileged group members are described as societal norms—as the way things are and as what is normal in society.[7] This normalization of privilege means that members of society are judged, and succeed or fail, measured against the characteristics that are held by those privileged. The privileged characteristic is the norm; those who stand outside are the aberrant or "alternative."

For example, a thirteen-year-old girl who aspires to be a major-league ballplayer can have only a low expectation of achieving that goal, no matter how superior a batter and fielder she is. Maleness is the foremost "qualification" of major-league baseball players. Similarly, those who legally are permitted to marry are heterosexual. A gay or lesbian couple, prepared to make a life commitment, cannot cross the threshold of qualification to be married.

I had an example of being outside the norm recently when I was called to jury service. Jurors are expected to serve until 5 P.M. During that year, my family's life was set up so that I picked up my children after school at 2:40 and made sure that they got to various activities. If courtroom life were designed to privilege my needs, then there would have been an afternoon recess to honor children. But in this culture children's lives and the lives of their caretakers are the alternative or other, and we must conform to the norm.

Even as these child care needs were outside the norm, I was privileged economically to be able to meet my children's needs. What many would have described as mothering, not privilege—my ability to pick them up and be present in their after-school lives—was a benefit of my association with privilege.

Members of the privileged group gain many benefits by their affiliation with the dominant side of the power system. This affiliation with power is not identified as such; often it may be transformed into and presented as individual merit. Legacy admissions at elite colleges and professional schools are perceived to be merit-based, when this process of identification with power and transmutation into qualifications occurs. Achievements by members of the privileged group are viewed as the result of individual effort, rather than privilege. . . .

B. CHOOSING WHETHER TO STRUGGLE AGAINST OPPRESSION

Members of privileged groups can opt out of struggles against oppression if they choose. Often this privilege may be exercised by silence. At the same time that I was the outsider in jury service, I was also a privileged insider. During *voir dire*, each prospective juror was asked to introduce herself or himself. The plaintiff's and defendant's attorneys then asked additional questions. I watched the defense attorney, during voir dire, ask each Asian-looking male prospective juror if he spoke English. No one else was asked. The judge did nothing. The Asian American man sitting next to me smiled and flinched as he was asked the questions. I wondered how many times in his life he had been made to answer such a question. I considered beginning my own questioning by saying, "I'm Stephanie

Wildman, I'm a professor of law, and yes, I speak English." I wanted to focus attention on the subordinating conduct of the attorney, but I did not. I exercised my white privilege by my silence. I exercised my privilege to opt out of engagement, even though this choice may not always be consciously made by someone with privilege.

Depending on the number of privileges someone has, she or he may experience the power of choosing the types of struggles in which to engage. Even this choice may be masked as an identification with oppression, thereby making the privilege that enables the choice invisible.

. . . Privilege is not visible to its holder; it is merely there, a part of the world, a way of life, simply the way things are. Others have a *lack,* an absence, a deficiency.

SYSTEMS OF PRIVILEGE

Although different privileges bestow certain common characteristics (membership in the norm, the ability to choose whether to object to the power system, and the invisibility of its benefit), the form of a privilege may vary according to the power relationship that produces it. White privilege derives from the race power system of white supremacy. Male privilege[8] and heterosexual privilege result from the gender hierarchy.[9] Class privilege derives from an economic, wealth-based hierarchy.

* * *

VISUALIZING PRIVILEGE

For me the struggle to visualize privilege has most often taken the form of the struggle to see my white privilege. Even as I write about this struggle, I fear that my own racism will make things worse, causing me to do more harm than good. Some readers may be shocked to see a white person contritely acknowledge that she is racist. I do not say this with pride. I simply believe that no matter how hard I work at not being racist, I still am. Because part of racism is systemic, I benefit from the privilege that I am struggling to see.

Whites do not look at the world through a filter of racial awareness, even though whites are, of course, members of a race. The power to ignore race, when white is the race, is a privilege, a societal advantage. The term "racism/white supremacy" emphasizes the link between discriminatory racism and the privilege held by whites to ignore their own race.

As bell hooks explains, liberal whites do not see themselves as prejudiced or interested in domination through coercion, yet "they cannot recognize the ways their actions support and affirm the very structure of racist domination and oppression that they profess to wish to see eradicated."[10] The perpetuation of white supremacy is racist.

All whites are racist in this use of the term, because we benefit from systemic white privilege. Generally whites think of racism as voluntary, intentional conduct, done by horrible others. Whites spend a lot of time trying to convince ourselves and each other that we are not racist. A big step would be for whites to admit that we are racist and then to consider what to do about it.[11]

NOTES

1. See Marilyn Frye, The Politics of Reality: Essays in Feminist Theory 19–34 (1983) (discussing sex marking, sex announcing, and the necessity to determine gender).

2. Angela Harris and Marge Shultz, *"A(nother) Critique of Pure Reason": Toward Civic Virtue in Legal Education*, 45 Stan. L. Rev. 1773, 1796 (1993).

3. Anne Fausto-Sterling, *The Five Sexes: Why Male and Female Are Not Enough*, Sciences, Mar./Apr. 1993. (Thanks to Gregg Bryan for calling my attention to this article.) See also Frye, *supra* note 1, at 25.

4. Adrienne Rich, *Compulsory Heterosexuality and Lesbian Existence*, in Blood, Bread, and Poetry, Selected Prose 1979–1985 (1986).

5. See Stephanie M. Wildman and Becky Wildman-Tobriner, *Sex Roles Iced Popular Team?* S.F. Chron., Feb. 25, 1994, at A23.

6. Rich, *supra* note 4, at 57 ("Heterosexuality has been both forcibly and subliminally imposed on women").

7. Richard Delgado and Jean Stefancic, *Pornography and Harm to Women: "No Empirical Evidence?"* 53 Ohio St. L. J. 1037 (1992) (describing this "way things are." Because the norm or reality is perceived as including these benefits, the privileges are not visible.)

8. Catharine A. MacKinnon, Toward a Feminist Theory of the State 224 (1989).

9. Sylvia Law, *Homosexuality and the Social Meaning of Gender*, 1988 Wis. L. Rev. 187, 197 (1988); Marc Fajer, *Can Two Real Men Eat Quiche Together? Storytelling, Gender-Role Stereotypes, and Legal Protection for Lesbians and Gay Men*, 46 U. Miami L. Rev. 511, 617 (1992). Both articles describe heterosexism as a form of gender oppression.

10. bell hooks, *overcoming white supremacy: a comment*, in Talking Back: Thinking Feminist, Thinking Black 113 (1989).

11. See also Jerome McCristal Culp Jr., *Water Buffalo and Diversity: Naming Names and Reclaiming the Racial Discourse*, 26 Conn. L. Rev. 209 (1993) (urging people to name racism as racism).

chapter two 2

Privilege as Paradox

–Allan G. Johnson

Regardless of which group we're talking about, privilege generally allows people to assume a certain level of acceptance, inclusion, and respect in the world, to operate within a relatively wide comfort zone. Privilege increases the odds of having things your own way, of being able to set the agenda in a social situation and determine the rules and standards and how they're applied. Privilege grants the cultural authority to make judgments about others and to have those judgments stick. It allows people to define reality and to have prevailing definitions of reality fit their experience. Privilege means being able to decide who gets taken seriously, who receives attention, who is accountable to whom and for what. And it grants a presumption of superiority and social permission to act on that presumption without having to worry about being challenged.

PRIVILEGE AS PARADOX

Individuals are the ones who experience privilege or the lack of it, but individuals aren't what is actually privileged. Instead, privilege is defined in relation to a group or social category. In other words, race privilege is more about *white* people than it is about white *people*. I'm not race privileged because of who I am as a person. Whiteness is privileged in this society, and I have access to that privilege only when people identify me as belonging to the category "white." I do or don't receive race privilege based on which category people put me in without their knowing a single other thing about me.

This means that you don't actually have to be white or male or heterosexual to receive the privilege attached to those categories. All you have to do is convince people you belong to the appropriate category. The film *Shakespeare in Love,* for example, is set in Elizabethan England, where acting on the stage was a privilege reserved for men. The character Viola (the woman Shakespeare falls in love with) wants more than anything to act on the stage, and finally realizes her dream not by changing her sex and becoming a man, but by successfully presenting herself as one. That's all that it takes.

In similar ways, you can lose privilege if people think you don't belong to a particular category. My sexual orientation is heterosexual, for example, which entitles me to heterosexual privilege, but only if people identify me as heterosexual. If I were to announce to everyone that I'm gay, I would immediately lose my access to heterosexual privilege (unless people refused to believe me), even though I would still be, in fact, a heterosexual person. As Charlotte Bunch put it, "If you don't have a sense of what privilege is, I suggest that you go home and announce to everybody that you know—a roommate, your family, the people you work with—that you're a queer. Try being queer for a week."[1] When it comes to privilege, then, it doesn't really matter who we really are. What matters is who other people *think* we are, which is to say, the social categories they put us in.

Several important consequences follow from this paradox of privileges. First, privilege is rooted in societies and organizations as much as it's rooted in people's personalities and how they perceive and react to one another. This means that doing something about the problem of privilege takes more than changing individuals. As Harry Brod wrote about gender privilege:

> We need to be clear that there is no such thing as giving up one's privilege to be "outside" the system. One is always *in* the system. The only question is whether one is part of the system in a way which challenges or strengthens the status quo. Privilege is not something I *take* and which I therefore have the option of *not* taking. It is something that society *gives* me, and unless I change the institutions which give it to me, they will continue to give it, and I will continue to *have* it, however noble and egalitarian my intentions.[2]

Societies and organizations promote privilege in complicated ways. We don't have to be special or even feel special in order to have access to privilege, because privilege doesn't derive from who we are or what we've done. It is a social arrangement that depends on which category we happen to be sorted into by other people and how they treat us as a result.

The paradoxical experience of *being* privileged without *feeling* privileged is a second consequence of the fact that privilege is more about social categories than who people are. It has to do primarily with the people we use as standards of comparison—what sociologists call "reference groups." We use reference groups to construct a sense of how good or bad, high or low we are in the scheme of things. To do this, we usually don't look downward in the social hierarchy but to people we identify as being on the same level as or on a higher level than our own. So pointing out to someone in the United States who lives in poverty that they're better off than impoverished people in India doesn't make them feel much better, because people in the United States don't use Indians as a reference group. Instead, they will compare themselves with those who seem like them in key respects and see if they're doing better or worse than *them*.

Since being white is valued in this society, whites will tend to compare themselves with other whites, not with people of color. In the same way, men will tend to compare themselves with other men and not with women. What this means, however, is that whites will tend not to feel privileged *by their race* when they compare themselves with their reference group, because their reference group is also white. In the same way, men won't feel privileged *by their gender* in comparison with other men, because gender doesn't elevate them above other *men*. A partial exception to this is the hierarchy that exists among men between heterosexuals and homosexuals: heterosexual men are more likely to consider themselves "real men" and therefore socially valued above gay men. But even here, the mere fact of being male isn't experienced as a form of privilege, because gay men are also male.

An exception to these patterns can occur for those who are privileged by gender or race but find themselves ranked low in terms of social class. To protect themselves from feeling and being seen as on the bottom of the ladder, they may go out of their way to compare themselves to women or people of color by emphasizing their supposed gender or racial superiority. This can appear as an exaggerated sense of masculinity, for example, or as overt attempts to put women or people of color "in their place," including by harassment, violence, or behavior that is openly contemptuous or demeaning.

A corollary to being privileged without knowing it is to be on the *other* side of privilege without necessarily feeling *that*. For example, I sometimes hear a woman say something like, "I've never been oppressed as a woman." Often this is said to challenge the idea that male privilege exists at all. But this confuses the social position of females and males as social categories with one woman's subjective experience of belonging to one of those categories. They aren't the same. For various reasons—including social-class privilege or an unusual family experience or simply being young—she may have avoided a direct confrontation with many of the consequences of being female in a society that privileges maleness. Or she may have managed to overcome them to a degree that she doesn't feel hampered by them. Or she may be engaging in denial. Or she may be unaware of how she is discriminated against (unaware, perhaps, that being a woman is the reason her professors ignore her in class) or may have so internalized her subordinate status that she doesn't see it as a problem (thinking, perhaps, that women are ignored because they aren't intelligent enough to say anything worth listening to). Regardless of what her experience is based on, it is just that—her experience—and it doesn't have to square with the larger social reality that everyone (including her) must deal with one way or another. It's like living in a rainy climate and somehow avoiding being rained on yourself. It's still a rainy place to be and getting wet is something most people have to deal with. . . .

OPPRESSION: THE FLIP SIDE OF PRIVILEGE

For every social category that is privileged, one or more other categories are oppressed in relation to it. The concept of oppression points to social forces that tend to "press" upon people and hold them down, to hem them in and block their pursuit of a good life. Just as privilege tends to open doors of opportunity, oppression tends to slam them shut.[3]

Like privilege, oppression results from the social relationship between privileged and oppressed categories, which makes it possible for individuals to vary in their personal experience of being oppressed ("I've never been oppressed as a woman"). This also means, however, that in order to have the experience of being oppressed, it is necessary to belong to an oppressed category. In other words, men cannot be oppressed *as men*, just as whites cannot be oppressed as whites or heterosexuals as heterosexuals because a group can be oppressed only if there exists another group that has the power to oppress them.

As we saw earlier, people in privileged categories can certainly feel bad in ways that can resemble oppression. Men, for example, can feel burdened by what they take to be their responsibility to provide for their families. Or they can feel limited and even damaged by the requirement that "real men" must avoid expressing feelings other than anger. But although belonging to a privileged category costs them something that may *feel* oppressive, to call it oppression distorts the nature of what is happening to them and why.

It ignores, for example, the fact that the cost of male privilege is far outweighed by the benefits, while the oppressive cost of being female is not outweighed by corresponding benefits. Misapplying the label of "oppression" also tempts us into the false argument that if men and women are *both* oppressed because of gender, then one oppression balances out the other and no privilege can be said to exist. So when we try to label the pain that men feel because of gender (or that whites feel because of racism, and so on), whether we call it "oppression" or simply "pain" makes a huge difference in how we perceive the world and how it works.

The complexity of systems of privilege makes it possible, of course, for men to experience oppression if they also happen to be people of color or gay or in a lower social class, but not because they are male. In the same way, whites can experience oppression as women, homosexuals, or members of lower social classes, but not because they're white.

Note also that because oppression results from relations between social categories, it is not possible to be oppressed by society itself. Living in a particular society can make people feel miserable, but we can't call that misery "oppression" unless it arises from being on the losing end in a system of privilege. That can't happen in relation to society as a whole, because a society isn't something that can be the recipient of privilege. Only people can do this by belonging to privileged categories in relation to other categories that aren't.

Finally, it's important to point out that belonging to a privileged category that has an oppressive relationship with another isn't the same as being an oppressive *person* who behaves in oppressive ways. That whites as a social category oppress people of color as a social category, for example, is a social fact. That doesn't, however, tell us how a particular white *person* thinks or feels about particular people of color or behaves toward them. This can be a subtle distinction to hang on to, but hang on to it we must if we're going to maintain a clear idea of what oppression is and how it works.

NOTES

1. Charlotte Bunch, "Not for Lesbians Only," *Quest* 11, no. 2 (Fall 1975).

2. Harry Brod, "Work Clothes and Leisure Suits: The Class Basis and Bias of the Men's Movement," in Michael Kimmel and Michael A. Messner (eds.), *Men's Lives* (New York: Macmillan, 1989), p. 280. Italics in original.

3. For a classic discussion of the meaning of oppression, see Marilyn Frye, *The Politics of Reality: Essays in Feminist Theory* (Trumansburg, N.Y.: Crossing Press, 1983), pp. 1–16.

chapter three 3

White Privilege: Unpacking the Invisible Knapsack
— Peggy McIntosh

Through work to bring materials from Women's Studies into the rest of the curriculum, I have often noticed men's unwillingness to grant that they are overprivileged, even though they may grant that women are disadvantaged. They may say they will work to improve women's status, in the society, the university, or the curriculum, but they can't or won't support the idea of lessening men's. Denials which amount to taboos surround the subject of advantages which men gain from women's disadvantages. These denials protect male privilege from being fully acknowledged, lessened or ended.

Thinking through unacknowledged male privilege as a phenomenon, I realized that since hierarchies in our society are interlocking, there was most likely a phenomenon of white privilege which was similarly denied and protected. As a white person, I realized I had been taught about racism as something which puts others at a disadvantage, but had been taught not to see one of its corollary aspects, white privilege, which puts me at an advantage.

I think whites are carefully taught not to recognize white privilege, as males are taught not to recognize male privilege. So I have begun in an untutored way to ask what it is like to have white privilege. I have come to see white privilege as an invisible package of unearned assets which I can count on cashing in each day, but about which I was "meant" to remain oblivious. White privilege is like an invisible weightless knapsack of special provisions, maps, passports, codebooks, visas, clothes, tools and blank checks.

Describing white privilege makes one newly accountable. As we in Women's Studies work to reveal male privilege and ask men to give up some of their power, so one who writes about having white privilege must ask, "Having described it, what will I do to lessen or end it?"

After I realized the extent to which men work from a base of unacknowledged privilege, I understood that much of their oppressiveness was unconscious. Then I remembered the frequent charges from women of color that white women whom they encounter are oppressive. I began to understand why we are justly seen as oppressive, even when we don't see ourselves that way. I began to count the ways in which I enjoy unearned skin privilege and have been conditioned into oblivion about its existence.

My schooling gave me no training in seeing myself as an oppressor, as an unfairly advantaged person, or as a participant in a damaged culture. I was taught to see myself as an individual whose moral state depended on her individual moral will. My schooling followed the pattern my colleague Elizabeth Minnich has pointed out: whites are taught to think of their lives as morally neutral, normative, and average, and also ideal, so that when we work to benefit others, this is seen as work which will allow "them" to be more like "us."

I decided to try to work on myself at least by identifying some of the daily effects of white privilege in my life. I have chosen those conditions which I think in my case *attach somewhat more to skin-color privilege* than to class, religion, ethnic status, or geographical location, though of course all these other factors are intricately intertwined. As far as I can see, my African American co-workers, friends and acquaintances with whom I come into daily or frequent contact in this particular time, place, and line of work cannot count on most of these conditions.

1. I can if I wish arrange to be in the company of people of my race most of the time.
2. If I should need to move, I can be pretty sure of renting or purchasing housing in an area which I can afford and in which I would want to live.
3. I can be pretty sure that my neighbors in such a location will be neutral or pleasant to me.
4. I can go shopping alone most of the time, pretty well assured that I will not be followed or harassed.
5. I can turn on the television or open to the front page of the paper and see people of my race widely represented.
6. When I am told about our national heritage or about "civilization," I am shown that people of my color made it what it is.
7. I can be sure that my children will be given curricular materials that testify to the existence of their race.
8. If I want to, I can be pretty sure of finding a publisher for this piece on white privilege.
9. I can go into a music shop and count on finding the music of my race represented, into a supermarket and find the staple foods which fit with my cultural traditions, into a hairdresser's shop and find someone who can cut my hair.

10. Whether I use checks, credit cards, or cash, I can count on my skin color not to work against the appearance of financial reliability.
11. I can arrange to protect my children most of the time from people who might not like them.
12. I can swear, or dress in secondhand clothes, or not answer letters, without having people attribute these choices to the bad morals, the poverty, or the illiteracy of my race.
13. I can speak in public to a powerful male group without putting my race on trial.
14. I can do well in a challenging situation without being called a credit to my race.
15. I am never asked to speak for all the people of my racial group.
16. I can remain oblivious of the language and customs of persons of color who constitute the world's majority without feeling in my culture any penalty for such oblivion.
17. I can criticize our government and talk about how much I fear its policies and behavior without being seen as a cultural outsider.
18. I can be pretty sure that if I ask to talk to "the person in charge," I will be facing a person of my race.
19. If a traffic cop pulls me over or if the IRS audits my tax return, I can be sure I haven't been singled out because of my race.
20. I can easily buy posters, postcards, picture books, greeting cards, dolls, toys, and children's magazines featuring people of my race.
21. I can go home from most meetings of organizations I belong to feeling somewhat tied in, rather than isolated, out-of-place, out-numbered, unheard, held at a distance, or feared.
22. I can take a job with an affirmative action employer without having co-workers on the job suspect that I got it because of my race.
23. I can choose public accommodation without fearing that people of my race cannot get in or will be mistreated in the places I have chosen.
24. I can be sure that if I need legal or medical help, my race will not work against me.
25. If my day, week, or year is going badly, I need not ask of each negative episode or situation whether it has racial overtones.
26. I can choose blemish cover or bandages in "flesh" color and have them more or less match my skin.

I repeatedly forgot each of the realizations on this list until I wrote it down. For me white privilege has turned out to be an elusive and fugitive subject. The pressure to avoid it is great, for in facing it I must give up the myth of meritocracy. If these things are true, this is not such a free country; one's life is not what one makes it; many doors open for certain people through no virtues of their own.

In unpacking this invisible knapsack of white privilege, I have listed conditions of daily experience which I once took for granted. Nor did I think of any of these perquisites as bad for the holder. I now think that we need a more finely differentiated taxonomy of privilege, for some of these varieties are only what one would want for everyone in a just society, and others give license to be ignorant, oblivious, arrogant and destructive.

I see a pattern running through the matrix of white privilege, a pattern of assumptions which were passed on to me as a white person. There was one main piece of cultural turf; it was my own turf, and I was among those who could control the turf. *My skin color was an asset for any move I was educated to want to make.* I could think of myself as belonging in major ways, and of making social systems work for me. I could freely disparage, fear, neglect, or be oblivious to anything outside of the dominant cultural forms. Being of the main culture, I could also criticize it fairly freely.

In proportion as my racial group was being made confident, comfortable, and oblivious, other groups were likely being made unconfident, uncomfortable, and alienated. Whiteness protected me from many kinds of hostility, distress, and violence, which I was being subtly trained to visit in turn upon people of color.

For this reason, the word "privilege" now seems to me misleading. We usually think of privilege as being a favored state, whether earned or conferred by birth or luck. Yet some of the conditions I have described here work to systematically overempower certain groups. Such privilege simply *confers dominance* because of one's race or sex.

I want, then, to distinguish between earned strength and unearned power conferred systemically. Power from unearned privilege can look like strength when it is in fact permission to escape or to dominate. But not all of the privileges on my list are inevitably damaging. Some, like the expectation that neighbors will be decent to you, or that your race will not count against you in court, should be the norm in a just society. Others, like the privilege to ignore less powerful people, distort the humanity of the holders as well as the ignored groups.

We might at least start by distinguishing between positive advantages which we can work to spread, and negative types of advantages which unless rejected will always reinforce our present hierarchies. For example, the feeling that one belongs within the human circle, as Native Americans say, should not be seen as privilege for a few. Ideally it is an *unearned entitlement*. At present, since only a few have it, it is an unearned advantage for them. This paper results from a process of coming to see that some of the power which I originally saw as attendant on being a human being in the U.S. consisted in *unearned advantage* and *conferred dominance*.

I have met very few men who are truly distressed about systemic, unearned male advantage and conferred dominance. And so one question for me and others like me is whether we will be like them, or whether we will get truly distressed, even outraged, about unearned race advantage and conferred dominance and if so, what we will do to lessen them. In any case, we need to do more work in identifying how they actually affect our daily lives. Many, perhaps most, of our white students in the U.S. think that racism doesn't affect them because they are not people of color; they do not see "whiteness" as a racial identity. In addition, since race and sex are not the only advantaging systems at work, we need similarly to examine the daily experience of having age advantage, or ethnic advantage, or physical ability, or advantage related to nationality, religion, or sexual orientation.

Difficulties and dangers surrounding the task of finding parallels are many. Since racism, sexism, and heterosexism are not the same, the advantaging associated with them should not be seen as the same. In addition, it is hard to disentangle aspects of unearned advantage which rest more on social class, economic class, race, religion, sex and ethnic identity than on other factors. Still, all of the oppressions are interlocking, as the Combahee River Collective Statement of 1977 continues to remind us eloquently.

One factor seems clear about all of the interlocking oppressions. They take both active forms which we can see and embedded forms which as a member of the dominant group one is taught not to see. In my class and place, I did not see myself as a racist because I was taught to recognize racism only in individual acts of meanness by members of my group, never in invisible systems conferring unsought racial dominance on my group from birth.

Disapproving of the systems won't be enough to change them. I was taught to think that racism could end if white individuals changed their attitudes. [But] a "white" skin in the United States opens many doors for whites whether or not we approve of the way dominance has been conferred on us. Individual acts can palliate, but cannot end, these problems.

To redesign social systems we need first to acknowledge their colossal unseen dimensions. The silences and denials surrounding privilege are the key political tool here. They keep the thinking about equality or equity incomplete, protecting unearned advantage and conferred dominance by making these taboo subjects. Most talk by whites about equal opportunity seems to me now to be about equal opportunity to try to get into a position of dominance while denying that *systems* of dominance exist.

It seems to me that obliviousness about white advantage, like obliviousness about male advantage, is kept strongly inculturated in the United States so as to maintain the myth of meritocracy, the myth that democratic choice is equally available to all. Keeping most people unaware that freedom of confident action is there for just a small number of people props up those in power, and serves to keep power in the hands of the same groups that have most of it already.

Though systemic change takes many decades, there are pressing questions for me and I imagine for some others like me if we raise our daily consciousness on the perquisites of being light-skinned. What will we do with such knowledge? As we know from watching men, it is an open question whether we will choose to use unearned advantage to weaken hidden systems of advantage, and whether we will use any of our arbitrarily awarded power to try to reconstruct power systems on a broader base.

chapter four

White Privilege/White Supremacy
—Robert Jensen

WHITE SUPREMACY

The United States of America at the beginning of the twenty-first century—a century and a half after the end of slavery, four decades after the passage of the Civil Rights Act—is a white-supremacist society.

By "white supremacist," I mean a society whose founding is based in an ideology of the inherent superiority of white Europeans over non-whites, an ideology that was used to justify the crimes against indigenous people and Africans that created the nation. That ideology also has justified legal and extralegal exploitation of every non-white immigrant group, and is used to this day to rationalize the racialized disparities in the distribution of wealth and well-being in this society. It is a society in which white people occupy most of the top positions in powerful institutions, with similar privileges available in limited ways to non-white people who fit themselves into white society.

That claim will strike many as ludicrous. Yes, we may have some remnants of racial inequality, and of course there are lingering racial tensions, and it's true that there are still some white people who hold openly racist beliefs. But white supremacist? The entire society? How can one make such a claim?

It's easy. We can start with the numbers. President Bill Clinton promised us a national conversation on race in the 1990s. The conversation didn't get very far, but his Council of Economic Advisors for the President's Initiative on Race did gather a large amount of data.[1] They detailed how, on average, whites are more likely than members of racial/ethnic minorities to:

- Attend primary and secondary schools with smaller class sizes.
- Have access to computer technology in public schools and at home during primary and secondary schooling.

- Attend and graduate from a four-year college or university.
- Earn higher salaries.
- Retain employment during a downturn in the economy.
- Be covered by health insurance and consequently gain access to health care.
- Survive certain life-threatening illnesses.
- Experience more favorable housing conditions (less crowding, less crime, less litter and deterioration, and fewer problems with public services).
- Spend a smaller percentage of household income on housing.
- Have unimpeded access to home mortgage loans and home ownership.
- Own stocks, mutual funds, and IRA accounts.
- Gain a substantial net worth.

If we look just at the statistics about blacks and whites, the numbers are stark. According to a 2004 study by United for a Fair Economy, on some measures black Americans had fallen behind white Americans in recent decades:[2]

- The typical black family had 60 percent as much income as a white family in 1968, but only 58 percent as much in 2002.
- One in nine African Americans cannot find a job. Black unemployment is more than twice the white race, a wider gap than in 1972.
- Black infants are almost two and a half times as likely as white infants to die before age one, a greater gap than in 1970.
- White households had an average net worth of $468,200 in 2001, more than six times the $75,700 of black households. In 1989 (the oldest comparable data available), average white wealth was five and a half times that of black wealth.

On many measures, closing the gap between black and white is decades, or centuries, away:

- At the slow rate that the black-white poverty gap has been narrowing since 1968, it would take 150 years, until 2152, to close.
- For every dollar of white per-capita income, African Americans had fifty-five cents in 1968 and only fifty-seven cents in 2001. At this pace, it would take blacks 581 years to get the remaining forty-three cents.
- Although white home-ownership has jumped from 65 percent to 75 percent since 1970, black home-ownership has only risen from 42 percent to 48 percent. At this rate, it would take 1,664 years to close the gap, after fifty-five generations.

- If current rates of incarceration continue, one out of three African-American males born today will be imprisoned at some point during their lifetimes.

- At the current pace, blacks and whites will reach high school graduation parity in 2013, six decades after the *Brown v. Board of Education* school desegregation decision. And college graduation parity would be reached until 2075, more than 200 years after the end of slavery.

What does white supremacy mean in day-to-day life? In the United States, a black applicant with no criminal record is less likely to receive a callback from a potential employer than a white applicant with a felony conviction.[3] In other words, being black is more of a liability in finding a job than being a convicted criminal. Studies show that from the mid-1990s through the beginning of the new century, such discrimination in low-wage jobs has remained constant. These statistics led the researcher to conclude that even if employers are not consciously discriminating against black applicants, "there are a lot of unconscious processes that come into play that bias or distort employers' perceptions of the quality or suitability of minority applicants."[4]

But numbers can never tell the whole story. The statistics have to be made real through the experiences and stories of people who live with the consequences of white supremacy. Such testimony of non-white people is readily available to anyone who wants to take the time to listen or read. If you aren't sure where to start, try something simple: Pick up a book or go online. Are you interested in the history and reality behind those statistics about black America? Try an anthology of important African-American writing, such as *Let Nobody Turn Us Around: Voices of Resistance, Reform, and Renewal.*[5] Or just type "driving while black" into an Internet search engine and read a few of the stories.

WHITE PRIVILEGE

In a white-supremacist society, white people will have privilege. That's hardly a radical claim, yet it continues to be controversial in many sectors of U.S. society. In 1986, Peggy McIntosh presented a paper that pointed out that although many white people were willing to acknowledge that racism put others at a disadvantage, they were less forthright about how that same system gives whites advantages of various kinds. Widely anthologized and republished,[6] the essay prompted discussion of white privilege in some circles, but such a simple assertion sparks considerable resistance from many white people.

White privilege, like any social phenomenon, is complex. In a white-supremacist society, however, all white people have some sort of privilege in some settings. There are general patterns, but such privilege plays out differently depending on context and other aspects of one's identity. So, it's true that a non-white manager can have power over a white employee who is in a subordinate position, and that a non-white person living in the upper-middle class enjoys a higher standard of living than a working-class white person. Class affects people's lives. It's also true that in this society men have power over women, and that power can cross racial lines. Gender affects people's lives.

But none of that derails a simple observation: In this white-supremacist society, whiteness consistently conveys certain privileges. A simple illustration of this was broadcast on the ABC News program "Primetime."[7] Using a hidden camera, the producers conducted a standard experiment to determine whether a white and black man would be treated differently in the world. Two men who worked for the Leadership Council for Metropolitan Open Communities in Chicago (a nonprofit group that works to ensure equal opportunity in housing) temporarily relocated to St. Louis, where they looked for an apartment, hunted for a job, shopped for shoes and cars, and went about the day-to-day business of living. The two men were alike in most every respect—age, education, background, work history—except race. In some situations, the men were treated equally. But a pattern of disparate treatment emerged, captured on video:

- The black man was ignored by salespeople in stores or tailed as a possible shoplifter, while the white man was greeted warmly and allowed to browse without suspicion.

- When both pretended to have locked their keys in their cars, the white man was showered with offers to help by passersby while the black man was ignored.

- At a used car lot, the white man was quoted more favorable terms for purchasing the same car.

- The white man was shown an apartment at a complex where the black man was told there were no vacancies.

- While the black man walked down the street in a predominantly white part of town, a white man leaned out of a passing car and said "Little far south, ain't it?" to let him know that he was in the wrong part of town.

All of that is evidence of white privilege. The anecdotal evidence of the program is backed up by statistics. But the real core of white privilege is revealed in the reaction of many white people to such a claim. When I showed the program to a class at the University of Texas, for example, a white student said, "The program isn't balanced. It shows the black guy getting harassed in a white neighborhood, but what would happen to me if I went to a black neighborhood?" Well, what would happen? Maybe a white man walking in a predominantly black part of town late at night would be at greater risk of being robbed or attacked than if he were black. Maybe. But even if that were the case, there are a few important differences. In most cases, white people can decide whether or not they want to go into a predominantly black neighborhood. In most cases, black people have no choice but to deal with a predominantly white world. If they want to get a job or secure a bank loan or buy a car, they will have to deal routinely with white people in a white world. The program we had just finished watching had detailed all the places where the black man had faced varying levels of discrimination or hostility. It was a difficult program to watch; the black man in the segment described the pain he felt, even though he knew it was "just a test." Yet instead of dealing with that, this white student in class had immediately raced to the one example he could think of—feeling unsafe walking in a black neighborhood—to begin the discussion. Or, more accurately, to try to end the discussion. That's part of white privilege—the privilege to ignore the reality of a white-supremacist society when it makes us uncomfortable, to rationalize why it's not really so bad, to deny one's own role in it. It is the privilege of remaining ignorant because that ignorance is protected.

There's one other disturbing aspect of that program, which I didn't notice until I had watched it several times. The show ends with one final illustration of discrimination: The two men go out on a New York street to catch a cab, with the black man standing in the foreground and the white man farther down the street. Both have their arms outstretched to hail a cab. Diane Sawyer, the reporter for this segment, points out that the first cab that pulls over glides past the black man and stops for the white man. The message is clear: In virtually every aspect of life—from the risk of racist violence, to getting a job, to finding a place to live, to the simple act of hailing a cab—the black person will face struggles and threats that the white person will not.

Cut back to the studio. Sawyer is at the desk, smiling happily. "We're going to motor on off ourselves," she says.

Such is television news; everything has to end on an upbeat note. But there was something incredibly depraved about the ending. After such a painful segment in which the white supremacy of the society was revealed, how could she smile? Even if such inanity is part of the script, how could she smile? How could she talk about "motoring off," making a bad joke that played on what we had just seen? Yes, I know, that's how television news operates. They smile, even when they have just finished reporting on a tragedy. But isn't there something sick about a white person delivering an indictment of white supremacy and then smiling? That's white privilege, too.

NOTES

1. Council of Economic Advisors, "Changing America: Indicators of Social and Economic Well-Being by Race and Hispanic Origin," September 1998. http://w3.access.gpo.gov/eop/ca/index.html.

2. United for a Fair Economy, "The State of the Dream 2004: Enduring Disparities in Black and White," January 2004. http://www.faireconomy.org/press/2004/StateoftheDream2004.pdf

3. Devah Pager, "The Mark of a Criminal Record." *American Journal of Sociology,* 108:5 (March 2003): 937–975.

4. Interview with Devah Pager, November 20, 2003. http://www.northwestern.edu/observer/issues/2003-11-20/newsfeed.html.

5. Manning Marable and Leith Mullings, eds., *Let Nobody Turn Us Around: Voices of Resistance, Reform, and Renewal* (Lanham, Md.: Rowman and Littlefield, 2000).

6. Margaret L. Anderson and Patricia Hill Collins, eds. *Race, Class and Gender: An Anthology,* 5th ed. (Belmont, Calif.: Wadsworth, 2004); Michael S. Kimmel and Abby L. Ferber, eds., *Privilege: A Reader* (Boulder, Colo.: Westview, 2003).

7. "True Colors," aired September 26, 1991.

chapter five 5

Membership Has Its Privileges: Thoughts on Acknowledging and Challenging Whiteness

– Tim Wise

Being white means never having to think about it. James Baldwin said that many years ago, and it's perhaps the truest thing ever said about race in America. That's why I get looks of bewilderment whenever I ask, as I do when lecturing to a mostly white audience: "what do you like about being white?" Never having contemplated the question, folks take a while to come up with anything.

We're used to talking about race as a Black issue, or Latino, Asian, or Indian problem. We're used to books written about "them," but few that analyze what it means to be white in this culture. Statistics tell of the disadvantages of "blackness" or "brownness" but few examine the flipside: namely, the advantages whites receive as a result.

When we hear about things like racial profiling, we think of it in terms of what people of color go through, never contemplating what it means for whites and what we don't have to put up with. We might know that a book like *The Bell Curve* denigrates the intellect of blacks, but we ignore the fact that in so doing, it elevates the same in whites, much to our advantage in the job market and schools, where those in authority will likely view us as more competent than persons of color.

That which keeps people of color off-balance in a racist society is that which keeps whites in control: a truism that must be discussed if whites are to understand our responsibility to work for change. Each thing with which "they" have to contend as they navigate the waters of American life is one less thing whites have to sweat: and that makes everything easier, from finding jobs, to getting loans, to attending college.

On a personal level, it has been made clear to me repeatedly. Like the time I attended a party in a white suburb and one of the few black men there announced he had to leave before midnight, fearing his trip home—which required that he travel through all-white neighborhoods—would likely result in being pulled over by police, who would wonder what he was doing out so late in the "wrong" part of town.

He would have to be cognizant—in a way I would not—of every lane change, every blinker he did or didn't remember to use, whether his lights were too bright, or too dim, and whether he was going even 5 miles an hour over the limit, as any of those could serve as pretexts for pulling one over, and those pretexts are used regularly for certain folks, and not others.

The virtual invisibility that whiteness affords those of us who have it is like psychological money in the bank, the proceeds of which we cash in every day while others are in a state of perpetual overdraft.

Yet, it isn't enough to see these things, or think about them, or come to appreciate what whiteness means: though important, this enlightenment is no end in itself. Rather, it is what we do with the knowledge and understanding that matters.

If we recognize our privileges, yet fail to challenge them, what good is our insight? If we intuit discrimination, yet fail to speak against it, what have we done to rectify the injustice? And that's the hard part, because privilege tastes good and we're loath to relinquish it. Or even if willing, we often wonder how to resist: how to attack unfairness and make a difference.

As to why we should want to end racial privilege—aside from the moral argument—the answer is straightforward: the price we pay to stay one step ahead of others is enormous. In the labor market, we benefit from racial discrimination in the relative sense, but in absolute terms this discrimination holds down most of our wages and living standards by keeping working people divided and creating a surplus labor pool of "others" to whom employers can turn when the labor market gets tight or workers demand too much in wages or benefits.

We benefit in relative terms from discrimination against people of color in education, by receiving, on average, better resources and class offerings. But in absolute terms, can anyone deny that the creation and perpetuation of miseducated persons of color harms us all?

And even disparate treatment in the justice system has its blowback on the white community. We may think little of the racist growth of the prison-industrial complex, as it snares far fewer of our children. But considering that the prisons warehousing black and brown bodies compete for the same dollars needed to build colleges for everyone, the impact is far from negligible.

In California, since 1980, nearly 30 new prisons have opened, compared to two four-year colleges, with the effect that the space available for people of color and whites to receive a good education has been curtailed. So folks fight over the pieces of a diminishing pie—as with Proposition 209 to end affirmative action—instead of uniting against their common problem: the mostly white lawmakers who prioritize jails and slashing taxes on the wealthy over meeting the needs of most people.

As for how whites can challenge the system—other than by joining the occasional demonstration or voting for candidates with a decent record on race issues—this is where we'll need creativity.

Imagine, for example, that groups of whites and people of color started going to local department stores as discrimination "tester" teams. And imagine the whites spent a few hours, in shifts, observing how they were treated relative to the black and brown folks who came with them. And imagine what would happen if every white person on the team approached a different white clerk and returned just-purchased merchandise, if and when they observed disparate treatment, explaining they weren't going to shop in a store that profiled or otherwise racially discriminated. Imagine the faces of the clerks, confronted by other whites demanding equal treatment for persons of color.

Far from insignificant, if this happened often enough, it could have a serious effect on behavior and the institutional mistreatment of people of color in at least this one setting: after all, white clerks could no longer be sure if the white shopper in ladies' lingerie was an ally who would wink at unequal treatment, or whether they might be one of "those" whites: the kind that would call them out for doing what they always assumed was acceptable.

Or what about setting up "cop watch" programs like those already in place in a few cities? White folks, following police, filming officers' interactions with people of color, and making their presence known when and if they observe officers engaged in abusive behavior.

Or contingents of white parents, speaking out in a school board meeting against racial tracking in class assignments: a process through which kids of color are much more likely to be placed in basic classes, while whites are elevated to honors and advanced placement, irrespective of ability. Protesting this kind of privilege—especially when it might be working to the advantage of one's own children—is the sort of thing we'll need to do if we hope to alter the system we swear we're against.

We'll have to stop moving from neighborhoods when "too many" people of color move in.

We'll have to stop running to private schools, or suburban public ones, and instead fight to make the schools serving all children in our community better. We'll need to consider taking advantage of the push for publicly funded charter schools by joining with parents of color to start institutions of our own, similar to the "Freedom Schools" established in Mississippi by the Student Non-Violent Coordinating Committee in 1964. These schools would teach not only traditional subject matter, but also the importance of critical thinking, and social and economic justice. If these are things we say we care about, yet we haven't at present the outlets to demonstrate our commitment, we'll have to create those institutions ourselves.

And we must protest the privileging of elite, white male perspectives in school textbooks. We have to demand that the stories of all who have struggled to radically transform society be told: and if the existing texts don't do that, we must dip into our own pockets and pay for supplemental materials that teachers could use to make the classes they teach meaningful. And if we're in a position to make a hiring decision, we should go out of our way to recruit, identify and hire a person of color.

What these suggestions have in common—and they're hardly an exhaustive list—is that they require whites to leave the comfort zone to which we have grown accustomed. They require time, perhaps money, and above all else, courage; and they ask us to focus a little less on the relatively easy, though important, goal of "fixing" racism's victims (with a bit more money for this or that, or a little more affirmative action), and instead to pay attention to the need to challenge and change the perpetrators of and collaborators with the system of racial privilege. And those are the people we work with, live with, and wake up to every day. It's time to revoke the privileges of whiteness.

People of Color Talk is Cheap

—Justin Podur

Any category or concept is going to leave important things out. It's the nature of abstraction. Using the term 'Black' to describe a group of people can obscure more than it reveals. As a biological category it is meaningless, as is the concept of race generally. There is no clear biologically relevant distinction between blacks and non-blacks. There are some genetic diseases, such as sickle-cell anemia, that are more prevalent among those with African ancestry compared to those with European ancestry. Other diseases prevalent in the Black community, like hypertension, however, are related to social, not biological phenomena.

Even as a social category, it abstracts a lot of differences. Within the group of Black people, there are men and women, there are children and adults, there are wealthy and poor, there are powerful and disenfranchised, there are those with access to resources and those without, there are those with legal status and those without. So a lot of detail and nuance is lost in the use of the concept.

Despite this, it is still very meaningful as a social category. Black people in the United States, for example, have less wealth, less income, suffer poorer health, and are disproportionately incarcerated compared to people who are not Black. To say that the concept of race has no biological value and that individuals are what they are, cannot be made into an argument to deny the social reality of racism. Racism is real. It is brutal. And in the system of caste that is US racism, Black people, and indigenous people, are at the bottom.

What about the concept of 'People of Color'? That, too, obscures a great deal. It obscures differentials in political power; it obscures class differences; it obscures gender differences; it obscures questions of imperialism; it obscures the crucial distinction in this world of those who have papers and passports and can cross borders and those who do not, cannot, and are 'illegal'.

Does it, however, have merit, like the concept of Black race or ethnicity, that countervails what it costs in abstraction? It has the merit of excluding whites, who, while they can be oppressed on gender or class lines, are at the top of the racial caste system. It can be a useful substitute for the term 'non-white'. But it can also lead to simple-minded analysis.

When whites in movements argue that everyone needs to get over race, transcend it, and work on common issues of class, against capitalism and the ruling elite, antiracists are unimpressed because such an approach enables the most privileged and powerful groups to impose their agenda on the rest. Such an approach denies problems of privilege and differentials of power within movements and organizations for social change. Denial is no basis for solidarity. As a substitute for denial, antiracists ask white activists to think about privilege, to be attuned to hierarchies and exclusion that can happen in organizations, and to work to overcome them. Pretending equality is already here is a recipe for maintaining inequality. Addressing and attempting to make structural redress for inequality can make a group, or a movement, stronger.

The way to fight racism is not to deny differences and hierarchies of privilege but to bring them out in the open and try to change them. But if that is the case, the 'People of Color' label is often not helpful, for several reasons.

First, because it leads to the same kinds of denial as comes from denying race altogether. There is a hierarchy of privilege within the group 'People of Color.' At the bottom are poor African Americans, indigenous people, and Latinos. At the top are an elite of people from different ethnicities selected and adopted into the ruling class. In between are groups of immigrants, some of whom have historically had a degree of upward mobility and are used against those below them as rhetorical devices: 'model minorities' who are supposed to have 'made it', proving that racism does not hold 'People of Color' back and thus that African Americans (as an example) have not 'made it' through their own fault. There are also groups of brutally exploited and oppressed immigrants and refugees, who work at low wages to try to remit money to support their families in poor countries under constant threat of deportation. These groups are treated differently within the racial system. They are subject to different stereotypes. They have different, and sometimes opposed, interests. Black people, for example, have an interest in a tighter labor market, while immigrants have an interest in the chance to go to the US to work. Many institutions, and often the law, think affirmative action obligations to Blacks to redress centuries of slavery and Jim Crow segregation and violence are met when an upper class Asian is hired.

Collapsing all of these groups under the rubric of 'People of Color' does exclude those at the top of the hierarchy (white people) but it leaves the rest of the hierarchy intact. As a result, people at the top of the new hierarchy—in movement organizations these are often drawn from the ranks of class-privileged academics from the least oppressed racial groups—can claim the oppression of everyone below them as their own. Rather than trying to understand and addressing our own privilege and hierarchy, we can posture and be righteous. This does not help those we ought to be most concerned about—those who are most oppressed, those who are at the bottom of the hierarchy.

If addressing privilege and working against it within social movements and organizations is onerous, then why should whites shoulder the burden alone, since they are not the only ones with privilege? If, conversely, as antiracists claim, addressing privilege and working against it is a positive personal growth experience, then why should whites monopolize such a wonderful thing? We could all benefit from understanding how privilege and hierarchy work, and taking an honest look at where we stand. Perhaps we could start by being a little more specific about the racial system and its impacts, which do not come down on everyone equally. Using a better set of categories might help. The categories I use for North America, with their own flaws and problems, are: European or white, South Asian, East Asian, West Asian, Latino, African or Black, and Indigenous, always with the question of citizenship and status (immigrant, refugee, status/non-status).

Recognizing these differences is particularly important when 'People of Color' groups, caucuses, and organizations are formed. A 'People of Color' caucus in a community antiwar group is an example. The idea here is good: to create an autonomous space where an oppressed group can work and develop without constantly negotiating boundaries and issues of privilege. So long as the creation of such a space does not come at the expense of representation of the oppressed in larger, integrated groups (in the antiwar example, the existence of a caucus should not prevent people of color from being represented in the leadership of the larger antiwar organization or coalition). But if the autonomous space is a 'people of color' space where highly privileged people of color interact with much less privileged people of color, the most oppressed still have no space, and can now be denied a voice, of their own.

It's true that no set of categories or concepts is perfect, and it would be easy to come up with arguments against the set I've chosen. But starting with a concept like 'People of Color', which obscures privilege and hierarchy within the racial system itself, can often make work harder for antiracists.

QUESTIONS FOR THINKING, WRITING, AND DISCUSSION FOR PART THREE

1. According to the essay by Stephanie Wildman and Adrienne Davis, what is a privilege? What forms or systems of privilege operate in U.S. society and how do they relate to each other?

2. The Wildman/Davis essay reports on an incident that occurred in a college class taught by a professor named Marge Shultz. Why did Professor Shultz call Mr. Rodríguez "Mr. Martínez"? Why is important to know that earlier in the day another professor had called him "Mr. Hernández"? Is it a big deal?

3. Select several sites or institutions in which you participate and analyze how privilege operates within each of them. For example, you might choose to examine several different classroom situations in which you have found yourself both in college and in earlier grades; you might look at privilege within your family and the families of friends or relatives; you might examine how privilege operates within a religious community to which you belong; etc.

4. What does Allan G. Johnson mean when he refers to the "paradox of privilege"? How does this paradox help explain why it is possible to *be* privileged without *feeling* privileged?

5. Peggy McIntosh wrote her classic essay on white privilege in 1988. In it she provides a listing of some of the privileges she "enjoys" as a white woman. Have things changed since she wrote her essays? How would you modify her list if you were making up a list of privileges that white people currently enjoy? Now create other versions of your list of privileges—versions that factor in class privilege and gender privilege. How about a listing of privileges people enjoy by virtue of their sexual orientation, their age, or their physical condition? After having made up these lists, go back and discuss your answer to question 1 above.

6. In his essay, Tim Wise uses the pronouns "we" and "our" frequently. Analyze his use of these words and the implications of defining "we" in the way he does.

7. Peggy McIntosh, Robert Jensen, and Tim Wise all discuss the privileges they enjoy as white people in contemporary U.S. society. How did you feel about each of these selections? Did you find any one of them more or less persuasive than the others? Why?

8. Language makes people see and not see how privilege operates. Evaluate how successful you think Podur is in making the reader question the effectiveness of using the phrase "people of color." What do you think is the value of using or not using this phrase?

9. How much money would you require, if you are white, to give up your white skin forever and live out your life as a Black person? Why?

part

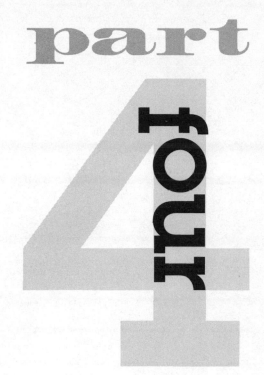

four

**whiteness:
the power of
resistance**

Breaking the Silence

—Beverly Tatum

Some people say there is too much talk about race and racism in the United States. I say that there is not enough. In recent years, news headlines have highlighted the pervasiveness of the problem. There have been race riots in Los Angeles and St. Petersburg, Florida. A thirteen-year-old Black boy was beaten into a coma by White youths who caught him riding his bicycle in their Chicago neighborhood. Anti-immigrant legislation in California has led to the public harassment of Latino citizens. Anti-Asian violence has increased dramatically. Precipitated by the damaging publicity incurred by the release of tape recordings in which Texaco officials used racial slurs to describe Black employees, Texaco agreed to pay $176.1 million to settle a race discrimination lawsuit, the largest such settlement in history.[1] Carl Rowan, a respected Black journalist, authored a book titled *The Coming Race War in America: A Wake-Up Call* in which he warns of the growing threat of White supremacist militia groups plotting to ignite racial conflict.[2]

What is happening here? We need to continually break the silence about racism whenever we can.[3] We need to talk about it at home, at school, in our houses of worship, in our workplaces, in our community groups. But talk does not mean idle chatter. It means meaningful, productive dialogue to raise consciousness and lead to effective action and social change. But how do we start? This is the question my students ask me. "How do I engage in meaningful dialogue about racial issues? How do I get past my fear? How do I get past my anger? Am I willing to take the risk of speaking up? Can I trust that there will be others to listen and support me? Will it make a difference anyway? Is it worth the effort?"

THE PARALYSIS OF FEAR

Fear is a powerful emotion, one that immobilizes, traps words in our throats, and stills our tongues. Like a deer on the highway, frozen in the panic induced by the lights of an oncoming car, when we are afraid it seems that we cannot think, we cannot speak, we cannot move.

What do we fear? Isolation from friends and family, ostracism for speaking of things that generate discomfort, rejection by those who may be offended by what we have to say, the loss of privilege or status for speaking in support of those who have been marginalized by society, physical harm caused by the irrational wrath of those who disagree with your stance? My students readily admit their fears in their journals and essays. Some White students are afraid of their own ignorance, afraid that because of their limited experience with people of color they will ask a naive question or make an offensive remark that will provoke the wrath of the people of color around them.

"Yes, there is fear," one White woman writes, "the fear of speaking is overwhelming. I do not feel, for me, that it is fear of rejection from people of my race, but anger and disdain from people of color, The ones who I am fighting for." In my response to this woman's comment, I explain that she needs to fight for herself, not for people of color. After all, she has been damaged by the cycle of racism, too, though perhaps this is less obvious. If she speaks because *she* needs to speak, perhaps then it would be less important whether the people of color are appreciative of her comments. She seems to understand my comment, but the fear remains.

Another student, a White woman in her late thirties, writes about her fears when trying to speak honestly about her understanding of racism.

> Fear requires us to be honest with not only others, but with ourselves. Often this much honesty is difficult for many of us, for it would permit our insecurities and ignorances to surface, thus opening the floodgate to our vulnerabilities. This position is difficult for most of us when [we are] in the company of entrusted friends and family. I can imagine fear heightening when [we are] in the company of those we hardly know. Hence, rather than publicly admit our weaknesses, we remain silent.

These students are not alone in their fear-induced silence. Christine Sleeter, a White woman who has written extensively about multicultural education and antiracist teaching, writes:

> I first noticed White silence about racism about 15 years ago, although I was not able to name it as such. I recall realizing after having shared many meals with African American friends while teaching in Seattle, that racism and race-related issues were fairly common topics of dinner-table conversation, which African Americans talked about quite openly. It struck me that I could not think of a single instance in which racism had been a topic of dinner-table conversation in White contexts. Race-related issues sometimes came up, but not *racism*.[4]

Instead, Sleeter argues, White people often speak in a kind of racial code, using communication patterns with each other that encourage a kind of White racial bonding. These communication patterns include race-related asides in conversations, strategic eye contact, jokes, and other comments that assert an "us–them" boundary. Sleeter observes,

> These kinds of interactions seem to serve the purpose of defining racial lines, and inviting individuals to either declare their solidarity or mark themselves as deviant. Depending on the degree of deviance, one runs the risk of losing the other individual's approval, friendship and company.[5]

The fear of the isolation that comes from this kind of deviance is a powerful silencer. My students, young and old, often talk about this kind of fear, experienced not only with friends but with colleagues or employers in work settings. For instance, Lynn struggled when her employer casually used racial slurs in conversation with her. It was especially troubling to Lynn because her employer's young children were listening to their conversation. Though she was disturbed by the interaction, Lynn was afraid and then embarrassed by her own silence:

> I was completely silent following her comment. I knew that I should say something, to point out that she was being completely inappropriate (especially in front of her children) and that she had really offended me. But I just sat there with a stupid forced half-smile on my face.

How could she respond to this, she asked? What would it cost her to speak? Would it mean momentary discomfort or could it really mean losing her job? And what did her silence cost her on a personal level?

Because of the White culture of silence about racism, my White students often have little experience engaging in dialogue about racial issues. They have not had much practice at overcoming their inhibitions to speak. They notice that the students of color speak about racism more frequently, and they assume they do so more easily. One White woman observed,

> In our class discussion when White students were speaking, we sounded so naive and so "young" about what we were discussing. It was almost like we were struggling for the words to explain ourselves and were even speaking much slower than the students of color. The students of color, on the other hand, were extremely well aware of what to say and of what they wanted to express. It dawned on me that these students had dealt with this long before I ever thought about racism. Since last fall, racism has been a totally new concept to me, almost like I was hearing about it for the first time. For these students, however, the feelings, attitudes and terminology came so easily.

This woman is correct in her observation that most of the people of color in that classroom are more fluent in the discourse of racism, and more aware of its personal impact on their lives than perhaps she has been. But she is wrong that their participation is easy. They are also afraid.

I am reminded of an article written by Kirsten Mullen, a Black parent who needed to speak to her child's White teachers about issues of racial insensitivity at his school. She wrote, "I was terrified the first time I brought up the subject of race at my son's school. My palms were clammy, my heart was racing, and I could not have done it without rehearsing in the bathroom mirror."[6] She was afraid, but who would advocate for her son if she didn't? She could not afford the cost of silence.

An Asian American woman in my class writes about the difficulty of speaking:

> The process of talking about this issue is not easy. We people of color can't always make it easier for White people to talk about race relations because sometimes they need to break away from that familiar and safe ground of being neutral or silent. . . . I understand that [some are] trying but sometimes they need to take bigger steps and more risks. As an Asian in America, I am always taking risks when I share my experiences of racism; however, the dominant culture expects it of me. They think I like talking about how my parents are laughed at at work or how my older sister is forced to take [cancer-causing] birth control pills because she is on welfare. Even though I am embarrassed and sometimes get too emotional about these issues, I talk about them because I want to be honest about how I feel.

She has fears, but who will tell her story if she doesn't? For many people of color, learning to break the silence is a survival issue. To remain silent would be to disconnect from her own experience, to swallow and internalize her own oppression. The cost of silence is too high.

Sometimes we fear our own anger and frustration, the chance of losing control or perhaps collapsing into despair should our words, yet again, fall on deaf ears. A Black woman writes:

> One thing that I struggle with as an individual when it comes to discussions about race is the fact that I tend to give up. When I start to think, "He or she will never understand me. What is the point?" I have practically defeated myself. No human can ever fully understand the experiences and feelings of another, and I must remind myself that progress, although often slow and painful, can be made.

A very powerful example of racial dialogue between a multiracial group of men can be seen in the award-winning video *The Color of Fear.*[7] One of the most memorable moments in the film is when Victor, an African American man, begins to shout angrily at David, a White man, who continually invalidates what Victor has said about his experiences with racism. After viewing the video in my class, several students of color wrote about how much they identified with Victor's anger and how relieved they were to see that it could be expressed without disastrous consequences. An Asian American woman wrote:

> I don't know if I'll ever see a more powerful, moving, on-the-money movie in my life! . . . Victor really said it all. He verbalized all I've ever felt or will feel so eloquently and so convincingly. When he first started speaking, he was so calm and I did not expect anything

remotely close to what he exhibited. When he started shouting, my initial reaction was of discomfort. Part of that discomfort stemmed from watching him just going nuts on David. But there was something else that was embedded inside of me. I kept thinking throughout the whole movie and I finally figured it out at the end. Victor's rage and anger was mine as well. Those emotions that I had hoped to keep inside forever and ever because I didn't know if I was justified in feeling that way. I had no words or evidence, solid evidence, to prove to myself or others that I had an absolute RIGHT to scream and yell and be angry for so many things.

The anger and frustration of people of color, even when received in smaller doses, is hard for some White people to tolerate. One White woman needed to vent her own frustrations before she could listen to the frustration and anger of people of color. She wrote:

> Often I feel that because I am White, my feelings are disregarded or looked down upon in racial dialogues. I feel that my efforts are unappreciated. . . . I also realize that it is these feelings which make me want to withdraw from the fight against racism altogether. . . . [However,] I acknowledge the need for White students to listen to minority students when they express anger against the system which has failed them without taking this communication as a personal attack.

Indeed, this is what one young woman of color hoped for:

> When I'm participating in a cross-racial dialogue, I prefer that the people I'm interacting with understand why I react the way that I do. When I say that I want understanding, it does not mean that I'm looking for sympathy. I merely want people to know why I'm angry and not to be offended by it.

In order for there to be meaningful dialogue, fear, whether of anger or isolation, must eventually give way to risk and trust. A leap of faith must be made. It is not easy, and it requires being willing to push past one's fear. Wrote one student,

> At times it feels too risky . . . but I think if people remain equally committed, it can get easier. It's a very stressful process, but I think the consequences of not exploring racial issues are ultimately far more damaging. . . .

NOTES

1. S. Walsh, "Texaco settles race suit," *Washington Post* (November 16, 1996).

2. C. A. Rowan, *The coming race war in America: A wake-up call* (Boston: Little, Brown, 1996).

3. In the same way, we need to break the silence about sexism, anti-Semitism, heterosexism and homophobia, classism, ageism, and ableism. In my experience, once we learn to break the silence about one ism, the lessons learned transfer to other isms.

4. C. Sleeter, "White racism," *Multicultural Education* (Spring 1994): 6.

5. Ibid., p. 8.

6. K. Mullen, "Subtle lessons in racism," *USA Weekend* (November 6–8, 1992): 10–11.

7. L. M. Wah (Producer/director), *The color of fear* [Video] (Oakland, CA: Stir-Fry Productions, 1994).

chapter **two**

Confronting One's Own Racism
—Joe Feagin and Hernan Vera

Most white Americans have absorbed racist attitudes from parents, friends, or the mass media. In this sense, racist views are a "normal" part of being a white American. Yet all whites can confront their racist views and propensities and seek to become egalitarian and antiracist. To understand the processes and dynamics of such change we and our students have conducted in-depth interviews and focus groups with whites who have taken antiracist steps or positions. In these interviews antiracist whites often acknowledge their own antiblack racism. The paradox of white antiracists openly acknowledging their personal racism is related to another paradox: that this realistic consciousness of a racist self liberates their expression of empathy for the oppression of black people.

For her research project in a racism seminar with Joe Feagin, graduate student Holly Hanson explored the racial attitudes of whites working to overcome racism.[1] One of the white women Hanson interviewed was once tied up by black thieves who robbed a store she was in. Yet she has refused to stereotype black people in general. She explained:

> I had spent many years before the incident nurturing friendships with black friends. So by the time the incident occurred, I had many black friends with whom I could talk intimately and honestly about my feelings. . . . We have to insulate ourselves with healthy relationships with people of other races to protect ourselves from the racist thought that is all around.

This woman had not come to her liberal views from a life of isolation. Rather, she and her husband have long made great efforts to develop friendships across the color line. Real friendships across the racial barrier have enabled her to withstand the daily drumbeat of racism all around her. In fighting the parochialism of white racism, antiracist whites actively seek out interaction with people in other racial groups. Most of the

151

antiracist whites with whom we and our students have talked have cultivated close friendships with black people in a variety of personal, church, and community settings.

The paradox that it is the antiracists who are most aware of their own racism and the racism of others can be seen in an answer this same respondent gave when she was asked if she considered herself colorblind:

> [I am] definitely aware of color. I think it is a superficial, comfortable response to, to denying one's own racism, and the problem of racism in society, to say that one has become colorblind. . . . The analogy that I frequently use is that, when people say, "Well, I just treat everybody the same and na-na-na," I say, If you know that a woman has been raped, you are liable to be careful, speaking to her. You are liable to be somewhat sensitive about how you approach certain things and really, when you think about it, your behavior at the end of your encounter with this woman probably is such that you should use it with everyone, you know, in a way. It is not ridiculous behavior. You are just going to be conscious of not wanting to put salt in wounds that you recognize probably are there because of that person's experience. . . . That is frequently the way I feel about interactions between blacks and whites in America. I think black people have been raped. I think they are raped, regularly, in a variety of ways.

Antiracist whites are not certain they can really understand the black experience, but many make an honest attempt. They admit that it is hard to understand the pain and anger. In another interview, a white male educator commented on the difficulty of understanding black anger:

> I think, yes, it is easy to accept a certain amount of anger. . . . I'm trying to construct explanations that help me understand, but I don't presume to understand from the point of view of having experienced in the same way as certain blacks who are angry might have experienced. So in that sense, no, I don't think it is easy to understand. . . . It takes a lot of effort, and a lot of time, and a lot of self-criticism on the part of the nonblack person.

This educator considers self-criticism a crucial part of the process of understanding. It is never easy, but, as he went on to explain, without it one becomes prey to wrongheaded assumptions about what is natural: "I think people who are in positions of power who are white and who are male need to learn . . . the subtle ways in which they convey messages of inequality and unequalness to others." Being white in this society almost by definition means rarely having to think about it. Whites must exert a special effort to become deeply aware of their own and others' racism. This educator was the victim of violence at the hands of blacks when he was younger, yet, like the woman above, he was able to process those incidents so the skin color of his assailants did not tint his larger view of the racism that afflicts U.S. society.

How do antiracists come to recognize and understand their own racism? For many a critical event or experience seems to catapult the matter of racism to the front of their minds. In an interview conducted by Hanson, a white teacher talked about what happened when she realized she gave support and attention to Latino toddlers and not to black toddlers where she once worked:

> And it was like I got hit with a bucket of cold water. And I thought, "Replay that one, Susan." And I replayed it in my mind, and I started to cry. And I cried and I cried, because I realized that *I had a prejudice.* And I thought I was without it. . . . So I went back, and I picked him up, and I played with him. I don't know, I sat him on my lap, and we did these little cutey games, patty-cake or whatever. And I had to work myself into it, because it was hard to do. It wasn't just a mental decision. "O.K., now I'm not going to be prejudiced any more." I did make a very strong effort, a concerted effort, to interact equally with all the children there. But I had to do it, I had to *make myself* do it. Because not only was I aware that it wasn't easy to do, once I knew that I was acting in a way that was prejudiced, I had to work very hard to overcome that.

A single important incident had focused her analysis of her own racist practice.

We have explored these critical incidents and events in our own research on antiracist whites. For two focus-group interview sessions, we invited several whites who had participated in at least one antiracist protest event. They had marched against the Ku Klux Klan, demonstrated against apartheid and racism, or appeared before city and county commissions in support of ordinances and policies designed to further human rights. They had taken a public stand against racism. A common thread uniting the focus group participants appears at first paradoxical: At one time or another, they all had to face the fact that they were themselves racist in thought or action. Most of the focus group participants associated their internal confrontation with their own racism with a triggering event or series of events in their lives.

One young woman related that she was raised by a father who was an official in the Ku Klux Klan. Her mother's marriage to this man was terminated when she was young, but not before she had adopted many racial dogmas of her father's group. Then, while still a teenager, she became pregnant by a white boyfriend and found herself ostracized by her white friends. Ironically, only the black students at school would associate and sympathize with her. When school officials barred her from attending classes because of her pregnancy, her black friends brought their notes and homework so she could graduate. This white woman's approximating experience of being ostracized because of her pregnancy not only gave her some experience with the pain of the "other" but also information that refuted her negative learned notions about blacks. Some years later, these critical experiences led her to become an active antiracist.

The events that led another participant, also a white woman, to an awareness of her own racism occurred when, as the wife of a U.S. soldier, she was forced to live in integrated housing for the first time in her life. She found a job in a place where most of the other workers were black. As a white southerner, these were dramatically new experiences for her. She developed a close relationship with her black neighbors and coworkers and came to know their pain from racial discrimination firsthand. She and her husband came to reflect on their role in inflicting pain on African Americans in the past. As a result, she became an antiracist activist. Working in Hawaii for a time, another focus group participant, a blond southerner, found himself in a community where most people were native Hawaiians. Some of the latter stereotyped him as a typical white Californian surfer, which he was not. Suffering from this stigma, he resisted anti-Hawaiian stereotypes and tried to establish close relations with some in the local community. As he struggled, he came to the realization that his position in Hawaii had some similarities to the condition of people of color in the whitewashed world of U.S. society. Once back in the United States, this reflection played a role in triggering his antiracist activities. All of these respondents belong to the group of whites who have gone beyond empathy for and understanding of what African Americans face and taken proactive stances to confront their own internalized racism and the racist views and actions of other whites.

TAKING ANTIRACIST ACTION

These responses make it very clear that an egalitarian and antiracist U.S. society is possible. There are already many antiracist whites in this country. Although they are usually not organized into antiracist societies, some whites do actively work to end racism. These include the people in our focus groups discussed above. All have worked for antiracist causes or participated in antiracist protests. Whether in protest demonstrations or in the workplace or neighborhood, such actions can mean risking one's privileges or resources. One of Hanson's white respondents described an incident at a store where she once worked:

> It was a simple matter of, well, I mean, it is my suspicion, that that is what happened. A black person was not hired for this job, and a white person was, and I challenged my boss about it because I was suspicious, and she said it was just schedules, it had nothing to do with that. But I noticed that in the next year she hired two black people whereas before that she had never hired anyone black before.

The willingness to risk one's job shows a strong commitment to a nonracist society. In another interview a white teacher discussed what whites should do for black coworkers who experience discrimination:

> The [black] social worker at the [social] services department that was my liaison person went through a real rough time, and I was an encourager, and I think a mentor, saying, "This is something that you do not have to just accept. You have options. Let's take a look at those

options. Let's get as much information as we can." It is like, like a good friend, willing to advocate for justice, or rights, or what's best for the person.

Antiracist whites have a different view of racial discrimination and of racial change than other white Americans. If they can come to a deeper understanding of racism, it is possible for many other whites to come to a similar understanding. The experiences of one of Hanson's interviewees led him to the strong conclusion that existing government programs are inadequate for changing racism in the United States. In his view, a realistic program of education for whites could get rid of racism in one generation:

> All prejudice could be removed in one generation if we had an education system that was completely united . . . to that end. Whose priority was not just . . . the increase in intellectual knowledge but the increase in spiritual knowledge. And what I mean by spiritual is not necessarily religious, but in knowledge of the true reality of human beings. And if we taught racial equality in the schools, if we taught it from the earliest age, and if we taught it in our churches, then obviously it would be removed in one generation.

One critical question is: How do we increase the number of these antiracist whites? Or, more generally, how do we go about getting rid of white racism in the United States? There are white Americans and black Americans currently working hard on these problems. For example, working with other antiracist activists, Nathan Rutstein, a white man, has set up more than one hundred local Institutes for the Healing of Racism. Rutstein utilizes a medical model in his work with community groups. He approaches racism as a white mental disease that leads to discrimination against people of color. Whites have a superiority complex covered up by denial and are afraid of exposing the deep prejudices most know are wrong. In his view whites are also victims of racism. Rutstein's approach emphasizes the oneness of all human beings. Multicultural training is not enough, for all Americans must come to see themselves as brothers and sisters. Every human being is in fact related to every other human being; each person is at least a fiftieth cousin of any other person on the globe. One major step forward in the antiracist cause is to integrate into all U.S. educational systems new courses on the oneness of all humankind.[2]

NOTES

1. We are indebted to Holly Hanson for permission to use excerpts from several interviews she conducted (in the Northeast and the Southeast) for her important work on the racial attitudes of people working to overcome racism.

2. Nathan Rutstein, *Healing Racism in America* (Springfield, Mass.: Whitcomb Publishing, 1993), pp. 1–51, 121–129.

How White People Can Serve as Allies to People of Color in the Struggle to End Racism

–Paul Kivel

WHAT DOES AN ALLY DO?

Being allies to people of color in the struggle to end racism is one of the most important things that white people can do. There is no one correct way to be an ally. Each of us is different. We have different relationships to social organizations, political processes and economic structures. We are more or less powerful because of such factors as our gender, class, work situation, family and community participation. Being an ally to people of color is an ongoing strategic process in which we look at our personal and social resources, evaluate the environment we have helped to create and decide what needs to be done.

Times change and circumstances vary. What is a priority today may not be tomorrow. What is effective or strategic right now may not be next year. We need to be thinking with others and noticing what is going on around us so we will know how to put our attention, energy, time and money toward strategic priorities in the struggle to end racism and other injustices.

This includes listening to people of color so that we can support the actions they take, the risks they bear in defending their lives and challenging white hegemony. It includes watching the struggle of white people to maintain dominance and the struggle of people of color to gain equal opportunity, justice, safety and respect.

We don't need to believe or accept as true everything people of color say. There is no one voice in any community, much less in the complex and diverse communities of color spanning our country. We do need to listen carefully to the voices of people of color so that we understand and give credence to their experience. We can then evaluate the content of what they are saying by what we know about how racism works and by our own critical thinking and progressive political analysis.

It is important to emphasize this point because often we become paralyzed when people of color talk about racism. We are afraid to challenge what they say. We will be ineffective as allies if we give up our ability to analyze and think critically, if we simply accept everything that a person of color states as truth.

Listening to people of color and giving critical credence to their experience is not easy for us because of the training we have received. Nevertheless, it is an important first step. When we hear statements that make us want to react defensively, we can instead keep some specific things in mind as we try to understand what is happening and determine how best to be allies.

We have seen how racism is a pervasive part of our culture. Therefore we should always assume that racism is at least part of the picture. In light of this assumption, we should look for the patterns involved rather than treating most events as isolated occurrences.

Since we know that racism is involved, we know our whiteness is also a factor. We should look for ways we are acting from assumptions of white power or privilege. This will help us acknowledge any fear or confusion we may feel. It will allow us to see our tendencies to defend ourselves or our tendencies to assume we should be in control. Then we will be able to talk with other white people so these tendencies don't get in the way of our being effective allies.

We have many opportunities to practice these critical listening and thinking skills because we are all involved in a complex web of interpersonal and institutional relationships. Every day we are presented with opportunities to analyze what is going on around us and to practice taking direct action as allies to people of color.

People of color will always be on the front lines fighting racism because their lives are at stake. How do we act and support them effectively, both when they are in the room with us, and when they are not?

It can be difficult for those of us who are white to know how to be strong allies for people of color when discrimination occurs. In the following interaction, imagine that Roberto is a young Latino student just coming out of a job interview with a white recruiter from a computer company. Let's see how one white person might respond.

Roberto is angry, not sure what to do next. He walks down the hall and meets a white teacher who wants to help.[1]

R = Roberto,   **T** = teacher

T: Hey, Roberto, how's it going?

R: That son of a bitch! He wasn't going to give me no job. That was really messed up.

T: Hold on there, don't be so angry. It was probably a mistake or something.

R: There was no mistake. The racist bastard. He wants to keep me from getting a good job, rather have us all on welfare or doing maintenance work.

T: Calm down now or you'll get yourself in more trouble. Don't go digging a hole for yourself. Maybe I could help you if you weren't so angry.

R: That's easy for you to say. This man was discriminating against me. White folks are all the same. They talk about equal opportunity, but it's the same old shit.

T: Wait a minute, I didn't have anything to do with this. Don't blame me, I'm not responsible. If you wouldn't be so angry maybe I could help you. You probably took what he said the wrong way. Maybe you were too sensitive.

R: I could tell. He was racist. That's all. (He storms off.)

What did you notice about this scene? On the one hand the teacher is concerned and is trying to help. On the other hand his intervention is not very effective. He immediately downplays the incident, discounting Roberto's feelings and underestimating the possibility of racism. He seems to be saying that racism is unlikely—it was probably just a misunderstanding, or Roberto was being too sensitive.

The teacher is clearly uncomfortable with Roberto's anger. He begins to defend himself, the job recruiter and white people. He ends up feeling attacked for being white. Rather than talking about what happened, he focuses on Roberto's anger and his generalizations about white people. By the end of the interaction he is threatening to get Roberto in trouble himself if he doesn't calm down. As he walks away he may be thinking it's no wonder Roberto didn't get hired for the job.

You probably recognize some of the tactics described. The teacher denies or minimizes the likelihood of racism, blames Roberto, and eventually counterattacks, claiming to be a victim of Roberto's anger and racial generalizations.

This interaction illustrates some of our common feelings that get in the way of intervening effectively where discrimination is occurring. First is the feeling that we are being personally attacked. It is difficult to hear the phrase "all white people," or "you white people." We want to defend ourselves and other whites. We don't want to believe that white people could intentionally hurt others. Or we may want to say, "Not me, I'm different."

There are some things we should remember when we feel attacked. First, this is a question of injustice. We need to focus on what happened and what we can do about it, not on our feelings of being attacked.

Second, someone who has been the victim of injustice is legitimately angry and they may or may not express that anger in ways we like. Criticizing the way people express their anger deflects attention and action away from the injustice that was committed. After the injustice has been dealt with, if you still think it's worthwhile and not an attempt to control the situation yourself, you can go back and discuss ways of expressing anger.

Often, because we are frequently complacent about injustice that doesn't affect us directly, it takes a lot of anger and aggressive action to bring attention to a problem. If we were more pro-active in identifying and intervening in situations of injustice, people would not have to be so "loud" to get our attention in the first place.

Finally, part of the harm that racism does is that it forces people of color to be wary and mistrustful of all white people, just as sexism forces women to mistrust all men. People of color face racism every day, often from unexpected quarters. They never know when a white friend, co-worker, teacher, police officer, doctor or passer-by may discriminate, act hostile or say something offensive. They have to be wary of *all* white people, even though they know that not all white people will mistreat them. They have likely been hurt in the past by white people they thought they could trust, and therefore they may make statements about all white people. We must remember that although we want to be trustworthy, trust is not the issue. We are not fighting racism so that people of color will trust us. Trust builds over time through our visible efforts to be allies and fight racism. Rather than trying to be safe and trustworthy, we need to be more active, less defensive, and put issues of trust aside.

When people are discriminated against they may feel unseen, stereotyped, attacked or as if a door has been slammed in their face. They may feel confused, frustrated, helpless or angry. They are probably reminded of other similar experiences. They may want to hurt someone in return, or hide their pain, or simply forget about the whole experience. Whatever the response, the experience is deeply wounding and painful. It is an act of emotional violence.

It's also an act of economic violence to be denied access to a job, housing, educational program, pay raise or promotion that one deserves. It is a practice which keeps economic resources in the hands of one group and denies them to another.

When a person is discriminated against it is a serious event and we need to treat it seriously. It is also a common event. For instance, the government estimates that there are over two million acts of race-based housing discrimination every year—twenty million every decade (Ezorsky, p. 13). We know that during their lifetimes people of color have to face many such discriminatory experiences in school, work, housing and community settings.

People of color do not protest discrimination lightly. They know that when they do white people routinely deny or minimize it, blame them for causing trouble and then counterattack. This is the "happy family" syndrome described earlier.

People of color are experts in discrimination resulting from racism. Most experience it regularly and see its effects on their communities. Not every complaint of discrimination is valid, but most have some truth in them. It would be a tremendous step forward if we assumed that there was some truth in every complaint of racial discrimination even when other factors may also be involved. At least then we would take it seriously enough to fully investigate.

How could the teacher in the above scenario be a better ally to Roberto? We can go back to the guidelines suggested earlier for help. First, he needs to listen much more carefully to what Roberto is saying. He should assume that Roberto is intelligent, and if he says there was racism involved then there probably was. The teacher should be aware of his own power and position, his tendency to be defensive and his desire to defend other white people or presume their innocence. It would also be worthwhile to look for similar occurrences because racism is usually not an isolated instance, but a pattern within an organization or institution.

Let's see how these suggestions might operate in a replay of this scene.

T: Hey, Roberto, what's happening?

R: That son of a bitch! He wasn't going to give me no job. He was messin' with me.

T: You're really upset, tell me what happened.

R: He was discriminating against me. Wasn't going to hire me cause I'm Latino. White folks are all alike. Always playing games.

T: This is serious. Why don't you come into my office and tell me exactly what happened.

R: Okay. This company is advertising for computer programmers and I'm qualified for the job. But this man tells me there aren't any computer jobs, and then he tries to steer me toward a janitor job. He was a racist bastard.

T: That's tough. I know you would be good in that job. This sounds like a case of job discrimination. Let's write down exactly what happened, and then you can decide what you want to do about it.

R: I want to get that job.

T: If you want to challenge it, I'll help you. Maybe there's something we can do.

This time the teacher was being a strong, supportive ally to Roberto.

I WOULD BE A PERFECT ALLY IF . . .

We learn many excuses and justifications for racism in this society. We also learn many tactics for avoiding responsibility for it. We have developed a coded language to help us avoid even talking about it directly. Our training makes it easy to find reasons for not being allies to people of color. In order to maintain our commitment to being allies, we must reject the constant temptation to find excuses for being inactive.

What reasons have you used for not taking a stronger stand against racism, or for backing away from supporting a person of color?

Following are some of the reasons I've recently heard white people use. I call them "if only" statements because that's the phrase they usually begin with. Our real meaning is just the reverse. We are often setting conditions on our commitment to racial justice. We are saying that "only if" people of color do this or that will we do our part. These conditions let us blame people of color for our not being reliable allies.

I would be a committed and effective ally:

■ If only people of color weren't so angry, sensitive, impatient or demanding;

■ If only people of color realized that I am different from other white people, I didn't own slaves, I treat everyone the same, I don't see color, I'm not a member of the KKK and I've even been to an unlearning racism workshop;

■ If only people of color would give white people a chance, hear our side of things and realize that we have it hard too;

■ If only people of color didn't use phrases like "all white people";

■ If only people of color didn't expect the government to do everything for them and wouldn't ask for special treatment.

Being a white ally to people of color means to be there all the time, for the long term, committed and active. Because this is hard, challenging work, we often look for ways to justify not doing it. Rather than finding ways to avoid being allies, we need to look at what gets in our way. Where does it get hard? Where do we get stuck? Many of the reasons listed above are ways to justify withdrawal from the struggle against racism.

Another way we justify our withdrawal is to find a person of color who represents, in our minds, the reason why people of color don't really deserve our support. Often these examples have to do with people of color not spending money or time the way we think they should. "I know a person who spends all her money on. . . . "

We often set standards for their conduct that we haven't previously applied to white people in the same position. "Look what happened when so-and-so got into office." In most instances we are criticizing a person of color for not being perfect (by our standards), and then using that person as an example of an entire group of people.

People of color are not perfect. Within each community of color people are as diverse as white people, with all the human strengths and failings. The question is one of justice. No one should have to earn justice. We don't talk about taking away rights or opportunities from white people because we don't like them, or because they don't make the decisions we think they should. Even when white people break the law, are obviously incompetent for the position they hold, are mean, cruel or inept, it is often difficult to hold them accountable for their actions. Our laws call for equal treatment of everyone. We should apply the same standards and treatments to people of color as we do to white people.

Not only are people of color not perfect, neither are they representatives of their race. Yet how many times have we said,

- "But I know a person of color who . . . "
- "A person of color told me that . . . "
- "So and so is a credit to her race . . . "
- (Turning to an individual) "What do people of color think about that . . . ?"
- "Let's ask so and so, he's a person of color."

We would never say that a white person was representative of that race, even if that person were Babe Ruth, Mother Teresa, Hitler, John Lennon or Margaret Thatcher, much less the only white person in the room. When was the last time you spoke as a representative for white people?

Imagine yourself in a room of fifty people where you are the only white person. At one point in the middle of a discussion about a major issue, the facilitator turns to you and says, "Could you please tell us what white people think about this issue?" How would you feel? What would you say? Would it make any difference if the facilitator said, "I know you can't speak for other white people, but could you tell us what the white perspective is on this issue?" What support would you want from other people around you in the room?

In that situation would you want a person of color to be your ally by interrupting the racial dynamic and pointing out that there isn't just one white perspective, and you couldn't represent white people? Would you want them to challenge the other people present and stand up for you? Being a white ally to people of color calls for the same kind of intervention—stepping in to support people of color when we see any kind of racism being played out.

BASIC TACTICS

Every situation is different and calls for critical thinking about how to make a difference. Taking the statements above into account, I have compiled some general guidelines.

1. Assume racism is everywhere, everyday.
Just as economics influences everything we do, just as our gender and gender politics influence everything we do, assume that racism is affecting whatever is going on. We assume this because it's true, and because one of the privileges of being white is not having to see or deal with racism all the time. We have to learn to see the effect that racism has. Notice who speaks, what is said, how things are done and described. Notice who isn't present. Notice code words for race, and the implications of the policies, patterns and comments that are being expressed. You already notice the skin color of everyone you meet and interact with—now notice what difference it makes.

2. Notice who is the center of attention and who is the center of power.
Racism works by directing violence and blame toward people of color and consolidating power and privilege for white people.

3. Notice how racism is denied, minimized and justified.

4. Understand and learn from the history of whiteness and racism.
Notice how racism has changed over time and how it has subverted or resisted challenges. Study the tactics that have worked effectively against it.

5. Understand the connections between racism, economic issues, sexism and other forms of injustice.

6. Take a stand against injustice.
Take risks. It is scary, difficult, risky and may bring up many feelings, but ultimately it is the only healthy and moral human thing to do. Intervene in situations where racism is being passed on.

7. Be strategic.
Decide what is important to challenge and what's not. Think about strategy in particular situations. Attack the source of power.

8. Don't confuse a battle with the war.
Behind particular incidents and interactions are larger patterns. Racism is flexible and adaptable. There will be gains and losses in the struggle for justice and equality.

9. Don't call names or be personally abusive.
Since power is often defined as power over others—the ability to abuse or control people—it is easy to become abusive ourselves. However, we

usually end up abusing people who have less power than we do because it is less dangerous. Attacking people doesn't address the systemic nature of racism and inequality.

10. Support the leadership of people of color.
Do this consistently, but not uncritically.

11. Don't do it alone.
You will not end racism by yourself. We can do it if we work together. Build support, establish networks, work with already established groups.

12. Talk with your children and other young people about racism.

NOTE

1. Adapted from *Men's Work: How to Stop the Violence That Tears Our Lives Apart* (Hazelden/Ballantine, 1992).

REFERENCE

Ezorsky, Gertrude. *Racism and Justice: The Case for Affirmative Action.* Ithaca, N.Y.: Cornell University Press, 1991.

QUESTIONS FOR THINKING, WRITING, AND DISCUSSION FOR PART FOUR

1. What kinds of reasons do the people quoted in Beverly Tatum's article give for being afraid to talk about race? Do you think these fears are broadly held in contemporary U.S. society?

2. If you are a white person, adopt the perspective of a person of color, and if you are person of color, adopt the perspective of a white person, and write an essay in which you discuss the fears and concerns that you believe such a person would bring to a discussion of race and privilege. Write your essay in the first person singular.

3. What do Feagin and Vera mean when they assert that "racist views are a 'normal' part of being a white American"? Do you agree or disagree?

4. In their selection, Feagin and Vera report on interviews with some white people who are working to overcome their racism. Select the example you find most interesting or most disturbing and talk about why.

5. Using as a model the scene between the student and teacher described in "What Does an Ally Do?" describe a racial incident in which you or a friend were involved, or which happened on your campus, or which you heard about from the news media, and write a scenario in which you explore what it would mean for a white person to serve as an ally to the person or people of color who were discriminated against.

6. In "I Would Be a Perfect Ally If . . ." Paul Kivel examines some of the excuses white people use to avoid taking responsibility for dealing with racism in U.S. society. React to these excuses. Can you think of additional excuses that white people use? Do you think any of these excuses are legitimate? Why? Why not?

7. What do you think race relations will be like in the United States ten years from now?

8. Identify five ways in which white people on your campus could challenge or undermine the ways white privilege operates there. Do the same with respect to the community in which you live and/or the workplace in which you work.

9. What do you think are the most compelling interests that people of color and white people share? Can they serve as the basis for people coming together across race difference and privilege to work for a common good?

Suggestions for Further Reading

Allen, Theodore. *The Invention of the White Race: Racial Oppression and Social Control,* Vol 1. London: Verso, 1994.

Babb, Valerie. *Making Whiteness Visible: The Meaning of Whiteness in American Literature and Culture.* New York: New York University Press, 1998.

Berger, Maurice. *White Lies: Race and the Myth of Whiteness.* New York: Farrar, Strauss, & Giroux, 1999.

Brown, Michael K., et al. *Whitewashing Race: The Myth of a Color-Blind Society.* Berkeley: University of California Press, 2003.

Bush, Melanie E. L. *Breaking the Code of Good Intentions: Everyday Forms of Whiteness.* Boulder, CO: Rowman & Littlefield, 2004.

Clark, Christine, and James O'Donnell (eds.). *Becoming and Unbecoming White.* Westport, CT: Bergin & Garvey, 1999.

Cuomo, Chris J., and Kim Q. Hall (eds.). *Whiteness: Feminist Philosophical Reflections.* New York: Rowman & Littlefield, 1999.

Dei, George Sefa, et al. *Playing the Race Card: Exposing White Power and Privilege.* New York: Peter Lang, 2004.

Delgado, Richard, and Jean Stefancic (eds.). *Critical White Studies: Looking Behind the Mirror.* Philadelphia: Temple University Press, 1997.

Feagin, Joe R., and Hernan Vera. *White Racism.* New York: Routledge, 1995.

Fine, Michelle, et al. (eds.). *Off-White Readings on Race, Power, and Society.* New York: Routledge, 1997.

Frankenberg, Ruth. *White Women, Race Matters: The Social Construction of Whiteness.* Minneapolis: University of Minnesota Press, 1993.

Hale, Elizabeth Grace. *Making Whiteness: The Culture of Segregation in the South, 1890–1940.* Vintage Books, 1999.

Hartigan, John, Jr. *Tribes: Toward a Cultural Analysis of White People.* Durham, NC: Duke University Press, 2005.

Ignatiev, Noel. *How the Irish Became White*. New York: Routledge, 1996.

Ignatiev, Noel, and John Garvey (eds.). *Race Traitor*. New York: Routledge, 1996.

Gallagher, Charles A. *Rethinking the Color Line*. New York: McGraw-Hill, 2004.

Jacobson, Matthew Frye. *Whiteness of a Different Color: European Immigrants and the Alchemy of Race*. Cambridge, MA: Harvard University Press. 1999.

Jensen, Robert. *The Heart of Whiteness: Confronting Race, Racism and White Privilege*. San Francisco: City Lights Books, 2005.

Kivel, Paul. *Uprooting Racism: How White People Can Work for Social Justice*. Philadelphia: New Society Publishers, 1996.

Lazarre, Jane. *Beyond the Whiteness of Whiteness: Memoir of a White Mother of Black Sons*. Durham, NC: Duke University Press, 1996.

Lipsitz, George. *The Possessive Investment in Whiteness: How White People Profit from Identity Politics*. Philadelphia: Temple University Press, 1998.

Lopez, Ian F. H. *White by Law: The Legal Construction of Race* (Critical America Series). New York: New York University Press, 1999.

McIntyre, Alice. *Making Meaning of Whiteness: Exploring the Racial Identity of White Teachers*. Albany: State University of New York Press, 1997.

Mills, Charles M. *The Racial Contract*. Ithaca, NY: Cornell University Press, 1997.

Morrison, Toni. *Playing in the Dark: Whiteness and the Literary Imagination*. New York: Vintage, 1993.

Nakayama, Thomas K., and Judith N. Martin (eds.). *Whiteness: The Communication of Social Identity*. Thousand Oaks, CA: Sage, 1999.

Painter, Nell Irvin. *The History of White People*. New York: W.W. Norton, 2010.

Rasmussen, Birgit Brander, et al. (eds.). *The Making and Unmaking of Whiteness*. Durham, NC, and London: Duke University Press, 2001.

Reddy, Maureen. *Crossing the Color Line: Race, Parenting, and Culture*. New Brunswick, NJ: Rutgers University Press, 1994.

Reddy, Maureen (ed.). *Everyday Acts Against Racism*. Seattle: Seal Press, 1996.

Roediger, David R. *Colored White: Transcending the Racial Past*. Berkeley: University of California Press, 2002.

Roediger, David R. (ed). *Black on White: Black Writers on What It Means to Be White*. New York: Shocken, 1997.

Rothenberg, Paula. *Invisible Privilege: A Memoir of Race, Class, and Gender*. Lawrence: University Press of Kansas, 2002.

Singley, Bernestine (ed.). *When Race Becomes Real: Black and White Writers Confront their Personal Histories*. New York: Lawrence Hill Books, 2004.

Sullivan, Shannon. *Revealing Whiteness: The Unconscious Habits of Racial Privilege*. Bloomington: University of Indiana Press, 2006.

Tatum, Beverley. *Why Are All the Black Kids Sitting Together in the Cafeteria? and Other Conversations about Race*. New York: Basic Books, 1997.

Tochluk, Shelly. *Witnessing Whiteness: First Steps Toward an Antiracist Practice and Culture.* Lanham, MD: Rowman & Littlefield Education, 2008.

Thompson, Cooper. *White Men Challenging Racism: 35 Personal Stories.* Durham, NC, and London: Duke University Press, 2003.

Trepagnier, Barbara. *Silent Racism.* Boulder, CO, and London: Paradigm, 2006.

TuSmith, Bonnie, and Maureen T. Reddy. *Race in the College Classroom.* New Brunswick, NJ: Rutgers University Press, 2002.

Wellman, David. *Portraits of White Racism.* Cambridge, UK: Cambridge University Press, 1993.

Williams, Gregory Howard. *Life on the Color Line: The True Story of a White Boy Who Discovered He Was Black.* New York: Dutton Books, 1995.

Williams, Linda Faye. *The Constraint of Race: Legacies of White Skin Privilege in America.* University Park, PA: Pennsylvania State University Press, 2003.

Wise, Tim. *White Like Me: Reflections on Race from a Privileged Son.* Brooklyn, NY: Soft Skull Press, 2005.

Wise, Tim. *Colorblind: The Rise of Post-Racial Politics and the Retreat from Racial Equity.* San Francisco: City Lights Books, 2010.

Acknowledgments

"The Matter of Whiteness," from *White: Essays on Race and Culture* by Richard Dyer, pages 1–10. © 1997. Reprinted by permission of Taylor & Francis Books UK.

"Failing to See," from *Racial Healing* by Harlon L. Dalton. © 1995 by Harlon L. Dalton. Used by permission of Doubleday, a division of Random House, Inc.

"Representations of Whiteness in the Black Imagination," from *Black Looks* by bell hooks. © 1992 by South End Press and Between the Lines Publishing. Reprinted by permission.

"History of White People" from *The History of White People* by Nell Irvin Painter. © 2010 by Nell Irvin Painter. Used by permission of W.W. Norton & Company, Inc.

"Sociohistorical Foundations of Whiteness," by Philip C. Wander et al., excerpted from Chapter 1 of *Whiteness: The Communication of Social Identity,* edited by Thomas K. Nakayama and Judith N. Martin. © 1999. Reprinted by permission of Sage Publications.

"How White People Became White," by James E. Barrett and David Roediger in *Critical White Studies: Looking Behind the Mirror,* edited by Richard Delgardo and Jean Stefancic. © 1996 by James E. Barrett and David Roediger.

"How Jews Became White Folks," by Karen Brodkin from "How Did Jews Become White Folks?" in *Race,* edited by Steven Gregory and Roger Sanjek. © 1994 by Rutgers, The State University. Reprinted by permission of the author.

"Becoming Hispanic: Mexican Americans and Whiteness," by Neil Foley from "Becoming Hispanic: Mexican Americans and the Faustian Pact with Whiteness" in *Reflexiones 1997.* Reprinted by permission of the Center for Mexican American Studies Books.

172

"The Possessive Investment in Whiteness," from *The Possessive Investment in Whiteness: How White People Profit from Politics* by George Lipsitz, Philadelphia, PA: Temple University Press. Reprinted by permission of the author.

"Global White Supremacy," by Charles Mills from *The Racial Contract.* © 1997 by Cornell University. Used by permission of the publisher, Cornell University Press.

"Making Systems of Privilege Visible," by Stephanie M. Wildman with Adrienne D. Davis from *Privilege Revealed: How Invisible Preference Undermines America* by Stephanie M. Wildman with contributions by Margalynne Armstrong, Adrienne D. Davis, and Trina Grillo, New York University Press, 1996. © 1995 by Stephanie M. Wildman. An earlier version was published in the Santa Clara Law Review, 35, 881 (1995). Reprinted by permission.

"Privilege as Paradox," excerpted from *Privilege, Power and Difference* by Allan G. Johnson. © 2001. Reprinted by permission of McGraw-Hill Companies.

"White Privilege: Unpacking the Invisible Knapsack," by Peggy McIntosh. © 1988 by Peggy McIntosh. Permission to duplicate must be obtained from the author: Excerpting is not authorized. A longer analysis and list of privileges, including heterosexual privilege, available for $6.00 from Peggy McIntosh, Wellesley College Center for Research on Women, Wellesley, MA 02181; (617) 283-2520, FAX (617) 283-2504.

"White Privilege/White Supremacy," from *The Heart of Whiteness* by Robert Jensen. © 2005 by Robert Jensen. Reprinted by permission of City Lights Books.

"Membership Has Its Privileges: Thoughts on Acknowledging and Challenging Whiteness," by Tim Wise. ZNET Commentary, June 22, 2000. © 2000. Reprinted by permission of the author.

"People of Color Talk is Cheap," by Justin Podur from *Z MAGAZINE.* © 2005. Jusin Podur is a Toronto-based activist and writer.

"Breaking the Silence," by Beverly Daniel Tatum from *Why Are All the Black Kids Sitting Together in the Cafeteria?* © 1997 by Beverly Daniel Tatum. Reprinted by permission of Basic Books, a member of Perseus Books, LLC.

"Confronting One's Own Racism," from *White Racism: The Basics* by Joe R. Feagin and Hernan Vera. © 1995. Reprinted by permission of Routledge, Inc., a part of The Taylor & Francis Group.

"How White People Can Serve as Allies to People of Color in the Struggle to End Racism," from *Uprooting Racism: How White People Can Work for Racial Justice* by Paul Kivel. © 1996 by New Society Publishers, Gabriela Island, British Columbia, Canada. Reprinted by permission.

Index

A

abolitionist movement, 36–37

"Act concerning servants and slaves," 48

affirmative action
G.I. Bill as, 46, 51
increased criticism of, 86–87
Scalia on, 88
in university admissions, for athletes and alumni children, 49, 111

Africa, colonialism in, 35, 96, 97

"African American" as term
as ethnic vs. racial label, 17
vs. other terms, 29

African Americans
attitudes to American wars, 100
current statistics, 128–129
drop in income of, 85–86
enslavement of, 72
environmental hazard exposure, 77–78
"feeble-mindedness" of, 47
FHA mortgages and, 76
as G.I.s, 53–54
health care of, 77–78
hostility toward, and whitening, 60, 65
Mexican Americans' attitudes toward, 60
in post–World War II labor force, 53

terrorizing of, 19–23
as three-fifths of a person, 35
urban renewal and, 75
as U.S. citizens, 61
wartime racism against, 56n11

African Mexicans, 62

"Afro-American," as term, 29

Agency for Toxic Substances and Disease Registry, 77

Aguinaldo, Emilio, 100

Aid to Families with Dependent Children (AFDC), 84

air pollution, 77, 78

aliens, African Americans as, 60

allies, white people as. *See also* antiracist action
guidelines for, 162–165
what allies do, 157–161

Alpine race
intelligence of, 48
Madison Grant on, 47
mixing with Nordic race, 45

"American," being
being "just American" vs. being Chicano or Mexican, 66
equated with whiteness, 71

anthologies, 129

anthropologists
Boasian and Du Boisian, 55n1
racism of, in nineteenth century, 34

anti-immigrant sentiment
    fear of political radicalism and,
        46–47
    at turn of 20th century, 37
antimiscegenation laws, 64
antiquity, 29–30
antiracist action, 135–136, 154–155.
    See also allies, white people as
anti-Semitism, 45–50, 56n8
Arabs, Greek Americans perceived as,
    42
Aryans, Asian Indians as, 48
Asian Americans
    Chinese Exclusion Act, 37, 48
    citizenship eligibility of Asian
        Indians, 48, 63
    importance of ethnicity to Chinese
        Americans, 16
    social ranking of Japanese
        Americans, by whites, 42
    stunted growth among Asian and
        Pacific Islanders, 78
    vs. white ethnic "inbetween-ness,"
        40
    wartime racism against Japanese
        Americans, 56n11
Asian and Pacific Islanders, 78
Association of New England Deans,
    49
Atlantic Monthly, 48
Australian Aborigines, 98
Aztlán, 66

B
Bakke case, 88
Baldwin, James, 20, 133
Barton, Josef, 41
beauty, personal, 30, 31
Belgian Congo, 35
Bell, Thomas, 41
The Bell Curve (Herrnstein and
    Murray), 133
Benjamin, Walter, 72
Bingham, Sallie, 21
"black," as term, 29
blackness
    association with slavery, 29
    as defined by whiteness, 16, 65–66
    legal adjudications of, 31n1, 35, 37

Black Peril, 99
"black queens," 10
Black Wealth/White Wealth (Oliver and
    Shapiro), 81–82
blanqueamiento, 61. *See also* whitening
blockbusters, 76, 82
Boyle Heights neighborhood, 74
British Empire, 35
Brod, Harry, 116
Brown, Lee, 79
brownness, 66
Bryn Mawr College, 49
Buck, Pearl, 100
Bukowczyk, John, 41
Bullard, Robert D., 77–78
Bush, George H. W., 82
"bush of ghosts," 19
business loans, 51

C
Car Wash, 10
Catholics, 50
Caucasians
    racial classification and, 30, 63
    South Asians as, 48, 63
census categories
    of 1930, 48, 59, 63–64
    of 1940, 50
    of 1980, 59
    in Mexico, 61
challenging white privilege,
    133–136
China
    European worries about, 99
    Opium Wars and, 96
Chinese Americans, 16
Chinese Exclusion Act, 37, 48
citizenship, U.S.
    court cases, 63, 68n13
    LULAC and, 60
    Mexican's entitlement to, 62
    whiteness as more important than,
        61
"civilizing mission" of whites
    in nineteenth century, 34–35
    Swiss reenactment of, 20
Civil Rights Act
    reversal of gains of, 80
    viewed as ending racism, 86

class, social
  claimed gender or racial superiority
    and, 117
  European races and, 47
  meanings of race and, 30
  power systems and class privilege,
    109
class conflict
  industrialization and, 46–47
  post–World War II labor struggles
    and, 51–52
classical scholarship, 30, 31n2
classification, racial
  history of, 33–37
  of Mexicans, 59, 62–64, 68n9
  in Mexico, 61–62
  in U.S. vs. Latin America, 97
  varied attempts at, 30
class size, in schools, 127
Clinton, Bill, 127
cocaine, 79
colonialism
  in Africa, 35
  global white supremacy and, 95–101
colonizationists, 36, 37
"colored," as term
  in censuses, 55–56n6
  definition of, in Texas, 64
  vs. other terms, 29
The Color of Fear, 148
Columbia University, 49
The Coming Race War in America
    (Rowan), 145
communism
  Emma Tenayuca and, 66
  fear of political radicalism and,
    46–47
community
  ethnic heritage as source of, 16
  vs. individualism, 15
commuter costs, 82
computer facilities, 127
conferred dominance, 124–125
"cop watch" programs, 135
Corby, Hazel, 11
The Cosby Show, 12–13n2
"cosmic race," 62
cranial capacity, 34
Croatian Americans
  embracing of term "hunky" by, 41

  social ranking of, by "whites," 42
Croson case, 88
The Crying Game, 13n4

D
Darwin, Charles, 98
Davenport, Charles B., 47
Declaration of Independence, 95–96
decolonization, 100–101
de Gobineau, Arthur, 31
deindustrialization, 85–86
Department of Housing and Urban
    Development, 76
deportation, 47
depression psychosis, 51
Dien Bien Phu, 100
disenfranchisement, 42
dishonorable discharges, 54
Doctrine of Discovery, 97
Dollard, John, 41
domestic workers
  control of gaze of, 21
  excluded from Social Security Act, 74
  observations by, 19
Douglass, Frederick, 36–37
Dred Scott v. Sandford, 97
driving while black, 129, 134
drug arrests and convictions, 78–79
Du Bois, W. E. B., 37, 60, 101
Dyer, Richard, 22

E
Eastern European immigrants
  embracing of term "hunky" by, 41
  importance of ethnicity to, 16
  on Long Island, 50
  mestizos as inferior to, 62
  non-whiteness of, 39–43
  scientific racism and, 46–48
  social ranking of, by "whites," 42
  whitening of, 37, 40, 63, 65
Eastern European slave trade, 29, 30
Economic Justice and the U.S. Economy
    (Catholic Bishops), 33
economic prosperity, 50–51
Edsall, Mary and Thomas Byrne, 86
educational benefits in G.I. Bill,
    51–54
educational discrimination
  class size and computer facilities, 127

legacy admissions, in universities, 49, 111
school segregation, 62, 64–65, 83
working to change, 135–136
Ellis Island, 47
employment discrimination
G.I. Bill and, 51
Mexican Americans and, 59–60
race vs. criminal record, 129
in 1980s and 1990s, 83
seniority system and, 80
tax law changes and, 84
environmental hazards, 77–78, 91n26
equity, home, 80
Essay on the Inequality of the Races (de Gobineau), 31n3
ethnic heritage
as source of community, 16
vs. race, 16–17
eugenics, 47–48
Euroethnics. *See* white ethnics
European races, 45–49. *See also* white ethnics

F
fair housing laws, 75
Fanon, Frantz, 98
farm workers
malnutrition among, 78
Social Security Act exclusion, 74
"fashion queens," 10
fear, 145–149
Federal Housing Administration (FHA) loans
as affirmative action for whites, 55, 74–76
black G.I.s and, 53–54
home equity and, 80
feeble-mindedness, 47
Filipino Americans, 42
Fisher, Christopher David, 87, 88
food stamps, 78
free market thinking, 83
Frye, Marilyn, 108

G
Galton Society, 47, 55n4
garbage incinerators and dumps, 77, 78
Garvey, Marcus, 98

gaze, control of, 21
gender
category words, 108–109
as feature of world, 108
meanings of race and, 30
gender privilege
gender hierarchy and, 112
impossibility of opting out of, 116
individual perceptions of, 117–118
General Services Administration, 74
Georgakas, Dan, 42
German Americans, 56n11
"ghosts," 19
G.I. Bill of Rights, 51–55, 56n10
G.I. Forum, 61
"ginnies"
as non-whites, 39
origin of term, 41
Glazer, Nathan, 56n9
Goddard, Henry, 47
government offices, 82
Grant, Madison, 47, 62, 99
Great Depression, 51
Great 1919 Steel Strike, 41
Greek Americans
as non-whites, 41–42
whitening of, 63
Greeks, ancient, 30
"Greeks," as term, 42
growth, stunted, 78
"guinea," as term, 39, 41

H
hair texture, 34
Haiti, 96
Hanson, Holly, 151
Harmand, Jules, 97
Harris, Cheryl I., 88
Harvard University, 48–49
health care, 128
health statistics, 78
height, 34
heterosexual privilege, 108–109, 112, 116, 117
highway construction, 75–77, 82
Hispanics. *See also* Mexican Americans; "Mexican," as racial label; Mexicans (in Mexico)
air pollution and, 78
distinctions among, 16

Hispanics *(continued)*
  drop in income of, 85
  drug convictions, 79
  as "ethnic" but white, 59, 65
  in post–World War II labor force, 53
  urban renewal and, 75
home loans. *See* mortgages
"Homeplace: A Site of Resistance"
    (hooks), 23
honky, as term, 41, 43n4
hooks, bell, 10–11, 112
Horatio Alger stories, 50
hospitals, racial segregation in, 68n9
Housing and Urban Development
    Act, 76
housing conditions, 128
housing discrimination
  FHA loans and, 74–76
  Mexican Americans and, 59
  recent, 80–82
  in 1980s and 1990s, 83
Huginnie, Yvette, 42
humanism, 97
"hunkies"
  as non-whites, 39
  origin of term, 41, 43n4
hybridity, 11–12

I
Ibson, John, 12
"if only" statements, 163
imagery, racial, 9–12
immigrants
  nineteenth-century racism and,
    46–47
  whitening of, 63
immigration restriction
  Chinese Exclusion Act, 37, 48
  citizenship cases, 63, 68n13
  Henry Cabot Lodge and, 47
  Mexican Americans and, 64
  in 1920s, 48
Immigration Restriction League, 49
inbetween-ness, 40, 41, 43
incarceration rates, 78–79, 129
Independent School District v. Salvatierra,
    64–65
"Indian," Emma Tenayuca as, 66

Indians, American. *See* Native
    Americans
Indians, Asian, 48, 63
individualism
  blindness to systemic behavior and,
    87–88
  vs. community, 15
industrialization, 46–47
infant mortality, 128
inner-city housing, 74–76
intelligence tests, 47, 48, 49
invisibility. *See also* invisibility of
    whiteness
  black pretense of, 21
  of privilege, 107, 110
  white pretense of black, 22
invisibility of whiteness
  color-blind language and, 89–90n4
  need to understand, 71–72
  postmodernism and, 11–12
  race obliviousness of white ethnics
    and, 16–18
  ubiquity of whiteness and, 11
  whiteness as normative state, 10–11
  white supremacy and, 101
IRA accounts, 128
Irene, 10
Irish Americans
  importance of ethnicity to, 16
  on Long Island, 50
  whitening of, 37, 40, 61, 65
Isandhlwana, battle of, 100
isms language, 109, 149n3
Italian Americans
  as "guineas," 41
  Joseph Loguidice, 39
  as kind of Jew, 49
  lack of wartime racism against,
    56n11
  on Long Island, 50
  as non-whites, 42
  whitening of, 40, 63, 65

J
Japan, 96, 100
Japanese Americans
  social ranking of, by whites, 42
  wartime racism against, 56n11

Jefferson, Thomas, 95–96
Jews
    early assimilation of, 46
    federal programs and, 54–55
    as "guineas," 41
    history of U.S. anti-Semitism and,
        45–50
    mestizos as inferior to, 62
    as "niggers," 42
    whitening of, 37, 49–50, 63
Jhally, Sut, 12–13n2
"just American," being, 66
"just human"
    Cosby Show family as, 12–13n2
    powerfulness of being, 10, 12
    white liberals' belief in being, 21

K
Karabel, Jerome, 49
Keller, John, 52
Kiernan, V. G., 95, 99
King, Rodney, 87
Knox, Robert, 98
Kroll, Michael A., 79
Ku Klux Klan, 53, 153

L
labor, meanings of race and, 30
landfills, 78, 91n26
language, 107–110
Latin Americans. *See* Hispanics
layoffs, 80
lead poisoning, 77, 78
League of Nations, 97
League of United Latin American
    Citizens (LULAC), 60, 61, 66, 67
leaky category, race as
    "one-drop" rule and, 37
    whiteness and, 34
*Let Nobody Turn Us Around: Voices of
    Resistance, Reform, and Renewal,*
    129
Lewis, Justin, 12–13n2
Lichtenstein, Alexander, 79
Lincoln, Abraham, 37
Lipsitz, George, 61
loans. *See* business loans; mortgages
Lodge, Henry Cabot, 47

Loguidice, Joseph, 39
Los Angeles rebellion, 87
Lowell, A. Lawrence, 48–49
Lower East Side, 47
LULAC (League of United Latin
    American Citizens), 60, 61, 66, 67
lynchings, 53

M
Malay race, 63
Malcolm X, 89n1, 98
malnutrition, 78
media representations
    ubiquity of whiteness and, 11
    under-representation of non-whites
        and, 13n3
medical care, 78
Mediterranean race. *See also* Southern
    European immigrants
    intelligence of, 48
    Madison Grant on, 47
    mixing of, with Nordics, 45
meritocracy, U.S. as, 50, 56n9
mestizos, 61–62
Mexican Americans
    abolition of slavery and, 72
    attitudes toward blacks, 60
    "brownness" of, 66
    de facto segregation of, 59–62
    divisions between, 66–67
    LULAC, 60, 61, 66, 67
    as nonwhite, in 1930 census, 59,
        63–64
    racial classification of, 64–65
    urban renewal and, 75
    whitening of, 59, 65–66
    as whites in 1940 census, 50
"Mexican," as racial label
    feeble-mindedness and, 47
    Greek Americans and, 42
    LULAC and, 61
    stigma of, 60
Mexicans (in Mexico), 61–62
middle class
    assimilation of white ethnics into,
        50–51
    entry of blacks into, 54
    fragility of, in blacks, 94n73

minimum wage, 83–84
mixing, racial
    antimiscegenation laws, 64
    between blacks and Mexican
        Americans, 60
    dilution of Nordic race and, 45, 47
    Mexican attitude toward, 62
    in Mexico, 61–62
"Mongolian," "Mongoloid" race, 30,
    63
"mongrelization," 45
Morrison, Toni, 60, 61, 65, 89n2
mortgages
    as affirmative action for whites, 55,
        74–76
    current disparities, 81–82, 128
    G.I. Bill and, 51, 52
mulattos, Greek Americans as, 42
Mullen, Kirsten, 147–148
multiculturalism, 11–12
mutual funds, 128

N
National Aeronautics and Space
    Administration (NASA), 52
National Association for the
    Advancement of Colored People
    (NAACP), 60
Native Americans
    differences among tribes, 16
    Doctrine of Discovery and, 97
    enslavement of, 72
    environmental hazards and, 78
    "feeble-mindedness" of, 47
    heritage of, for Mexican Americans,
        66
    in Mexico, 61–62
    as non-whites, 37
    racialized history of U.S. and, 73
    Thomas Jefferson on, 95
    Valladolid Conference and, 97
natural selection, 98
"Negro," as term
    in census classifications, 56n6
    vs. other terms, 29
"Negro," "Negroid" race, 30, 63
"Negro problem," 71, 89n1
Nehru, Jawaharlal, 98

neighborhoods, segregated, 74–75
neoconservatives, 82–83, 86, 94n73
net worth, 81–82
New Deal, 51, 73–74, 90n9
New York Times, 47
"niggers," Jews as, 42
Nordic race
    intelligence of, 48
    race mixing as menace to, 45, 47, 62
normalization
    of privilege, 110–111
    of whiteness, 10–12
Notes of Native Son (Baldwin), 20
"not-yet-white" ethnics, 41
nutritional deficiencies, 78

O
obliviousness, race, 16–18
Oliver, Melvin, 81
"one-drop" theory, 37
Opium Wars, 96
oppression, misapplication of label,
    118
opting out of engagement, 111–112
"other"
    blacks as, 11
    recognizing pain of, 153
    whites as, 19–23
Out of This Furnace (Bell), 41
Ozawa, Takao, 63

P
Palmer raids, 46–47
Pan-Asiatic Greater East Asia Co-
    Prosperity Sphere, 99–100
The Passing of the Great Race (Grant),
    47, 99
Passion and Prejudice (Bingham), 21
Peck, Gunther, 42
"peon blood," 62
"people of color" rubric, 137–139
Polish Americans. *See also* Eastern
    European immigrants
    embracing of term "hunky" by, 41
    importance of ethnicity to, 16
    on Long Island, 50
    social ranking of, by "whites," 42
    whitening of, 40, 65

pollution, environmental, 77–78,
    91n26
Portuguese Americans, 41
postmodernism, 11–12
preferential hiring. *See* employment
    discrimination
presence of mind, 72
President's Initiative on Race, 127
"Primetime," 130–131
prisons
    cost to society of building, 134–135
    drug arrests and convictions, 129
    incarceration rates, 78–79
    racial classification of Mexicans in, 62
privilege. *See also* white privilege
    defining, 110–112
    invisibility of, 107, 110, 121–122
    language and, 107–110
    oppression as cost of, 118–119, 121
    paradox of, 115–118
    visualizing, 112–113
propertied, straight white males
    (PSWMs), 36
property
    European view of, 35
    whiteness as, 37, 63
Proposition 13, 84–85
Protestants
    construction of whiteness by, 67
    on Long Island, 50
    preferential university admission of,
        49
"proto-nothing," 40
PSWMs (propertied, straight white
    males), 36
psychological tests, 49
Puerto Ricans
    FHA mortgages and, 76
    Greek Americans perceived as, 42
    as "guineas," 41
    urban renewal and, 75

R
race
    category words, 108
    as feature of world, 108
raced and non-raced images, 10
race riots, 145

The Races of Men (Knox), 98
"race suicide," 47
race theory, 34–37
racial profiling, 133, 134
racism
    confronting one's own, 151–155
    as term, 109–110, 112–113
radiation, 78
Reagan, Ronald, 82
redevelopment projects, 84
Red Scare of 1919, 46
Rhodes, Cecil, 99
Rich, Adrienne, 108
*The Rising Tide of Color against White
    World-Supremacy* (Stoddard), 99
Roosevelt, Theodore, 47
Roots, 17
Ross, David, 51
Rowan, Carl, 145
Russo-Japanese War, 99, 100

S
San Jose Junior College, 52
Sawyer, Diane, 131
Scalia, Antonin, 88
Scarborough, William Sanders, 31n2
schools
    class size and computer facilities,
        127
    segregation in, 62, 64–65, 83
    working to change, 135–136
scientific racism, 46–48
"scramble for Africa," 96
segregation
    in federal civil service, 37
    housing and, 74–76
    of Mexican Americans, 59–62, 64
    in 1980s and 1990s, 82–83
    in schools, 62, 64–65, 83
self-criticism, 152
seniority, job, 80
Serbian Americans, 42
Seven Sister schools, 49
sewage facilities, 74
"sexism," as term, 109
Shakespeare in Love, 116
Shapiro, Thomas, 81
Shultz, Marge, 108

Sicilian Americans, 41
Silberman, Charles, 56n9
silence
  need to break, 145–149
  as political tool, 125
  as privilege, 111–112
  status quo and, 107
Silicon Valley, 52
Sitting Bull, 98
skin color. *See also* classification, racial
  association with slavery, 35
  early racial classification and, 34
  of Italian Americans, 42
  light-skinned slaves and, 36
  naturalization cases and, 63
  as passport, 97
  vs. race, 31n1
Sklare, Marshall, 56n9
slavery
  association of blackness with, 29
  "civilizing mission" of whites and, 35
  control of gaze and, 21
  destruction of African cultural
    heritage by, 17
  equated with blackness, 35
  possessive investment in whiteness
    and, 72–73
  racial inferiority and, 72
  seen as sole source of black
    grievance, 87–88
  Thomas Jefferson and, 96
  in U.S. history, 36
  worldwide perspective, 30
Slavs. *See* Eastern European
    immigrants
Sleeter, Christine, 146–147
Slovenian Americans, 41
Social Security Act, 74
Southern European immigrants
  "feeble-mindedness" of, 47
  mestizos as inferior to, 62
  non-whiteness of, 39–43
  scientific racism and, 46–48
  whitening of, 63
Spanish American War, 96, 100
Spanish people, in Mexico, 61–62
St. Louis, 74
steelworkers, 39, 41
stereotypes, raced and non-raced, 10
stocks, 128

Stoddard, Lothrop, 99
Stono Rebellion, 73
"Stranger in the Village" (Baldwin), 20
strict scrutiny standard, 88
strikes
  after World War II, 51
  Great 1919 Steel Strike, 41
  post–World War I wave of, 46
structure, social, 72
"subject races," 96
subordination, language of, 109–110
suburbs, segregated, 74–75
superfund sites, 77
Supreme Court
  on affirmative action, 88
  Dred Scott decision, 97
  naturalization cases, 48, 63
  on whitening of white ethnics, 63

T
Taney, Roger, 97
tax law changes, 83–84
"temporary Negroes," 41
Tenayuca, Emma, 65–66
terrorists, whites as, 19, 22–23
"tester" teams, 135
Texaco, 145
Thind, Bhagat Singh, 48, 63
"Third World," as category, 23, 101
Thomas, M. Carey, 49
Thompson, E. P., 40
toxic waste, 77–78, 91n26
Treaty of Tordesillas, 97

U
ubiquity and invisibility of whiteness,
    11, 71–72, 89–90n4
unearned advantage, 124–125
unemployment, 128
unions
  favoring of whites by, 74
  Reagan Democrats and, 83
urban renewal, 74–76, 80, 82
U.S. Employment Service, 53–54

V
Valladolid Conference, 97
Versailles Conference, 97
Veteran's Administration (VA)
    benefits, 53–55

Vietnamese Americans, 16
Vietnam War, 16
violence, racist, 53
voting, 42, 86

W
wages, 51
"wage" slaves, 36
Wagner Act, 74
War for Independence, 35
Waters, Mary, 61
water supplies, 74
West Indians, 16
"White" (Dyer), 22
white ethnics
    affirmative action for, 54–55
    New Deal coalition with southern
        whites, 90
    as non-whites, 39–43, 45
    race obliviousness of, 16–18
    vs. whiteness itself, 12
    whitening of, 37, 49–51, 75
whiteness. *See also* whiteness, legal
        adjudications of; whiteness,
        possessive investment in;
        whitening
    as absence of African ancestry, 64
    attempts at classification of, 30
    in black imagination, 19–23
    as defined by non-whiteness, 16, 33,
        65–66, 71
    historical views of, 33–37
    linguistic associations of, 22
    Mexican Americans' achievement
        of, 66–67
    Mexicans and, 59, 60–64, 65
    as non-raced, 9–12, 17–18
    northwest European ancestry and, 48
    property right in, 63
    racialization of "nonwhite" groups
        and, 73
    ubiquity and invisibility of, 71–72,
        89–90n4
whiteness, legal adjudications of
    Italian Americans and, 42
    Mexicans and, 62
    multiple efforts at, 35
    naturalization cases, 48, 63
    non-importance of skin color, 31n1

"one-drop" theory, 37
whiteness, possessive investment in
    after World War II, 74–77
    choosing the Caucasian option and,
        61
    drug arrests and convictions, 78–79
    environmental hazards, 77–78,
        91n26
    history, to New Deal, 72–73
    housing discrimination, 80–82
    New Deal and, 73–74, 90n9
    1980s and 1990s, 82–85
    whites' perceptions of, 85–89
whitening. *See also* whiteness
    blacks as "real aliens" and, 60
    G.I. benefits and, 54
    of Jews, 46, 49–51
    of Mexican Americans, 59, 65–66
    urban renewal and, 75
White Peril, 99
white privilege. *See also* privilege
    ABC "Primetime" program,
        130–131
    changing, 125
    complexity of, 129–130
    examples of, 122–123
    invisibility of, 121–122
    responsibility of whites to challenge,
        133–136
    as unearned advantage and
        confirmed dominance, 124–125
"white problem," 79, 89n1
white slavery, 30
white supremacy
    current statistics, 127–129
    extremist associations, 110
    global nature of, 95–101
    representations of African
        Americans and, 89n2
Wilson, Woodrow, 37, 47
World War I, 48, 99
Wray, Linda, 78
Wright, Richard, 79, 89n1
Wygant case, 88

Y
Yellow Peril, 99
Yerkes, Robert, 47, 48